We Are *Trophies* Of *Christ's Victory*

Xulon Press
2301 Lucien Way #415
Maitland, FL 32751
407.339.4217
www.xulonpress.com

© 2020 by Ineke Vandewetering

All rights reserved solely by the author. The author guarantees all contents are original and do not infringe upon the legal rights of any other person or work. No part of this book may be reproduced in any form without the permission of the author. The views expressed in this book are not necessarily those of the publisher.

Disclaimer: Ineke Vandewetering is not a physician and does not intend, by anything that she says in this book, to dispensing medical advice to the reader. She encourages each individual to seek God for their own avenue of healing. You should consult a physician before changing your medication or discontinuing any prescribed treatment. Any health advice adopted from this book by the reader is done at his or her own risk. If additional health advice is needed, seek the advice of your health professional. Neither the author of this book nor Xulon Press has any liability whatsoever in regard to loss, damage, or injury suffered directly or indirectly as a result of the information contained in this book

Unless otherwise indicated, Scripture quotations taken from the Amplified Bible (AMP). Copyright © 1954, 1958, 1962, 1964, 1965, 1987 by The Lockman Foundation. Used by permission. All rights reserved.

Scripture quotations taken from the Holy Bible, New International Version (NIV). Copyright © 1973, 1978, 1984, 2011 by Biblica, Inc.™. Used by permission. All rights reserved.

Printed in the United States of America.

Paperback ISBN-13: 978-1-6312-9378-8

Ebook ISBN-13: 978-1-6312-9379-5

Dedication

This book is dedicated to all of you who believe that Jesus Christ is the same yesterday, today, and forever!

Table Of Contents

Acknowledgments ix
Introduction xi

Part One:

**How Our Romance—
And My Romance With The Lord—Started** xv

1: A Prayer, A Dream, A Marriage 1
2: Confrontation With My Dad. 13
3: Forgiveness Brings Us Into Victory. 25
4: Our Lord Is Omnipotent! 37

Part Two:

We Are Trophies Of Christ's Victory 45
5: A Warning Through A Vision 47
6: Healed Forever! 57

Part Three:

She Will Not Die But Live 69
7: The Lord Is Good, Gracious, And Faithful. 71
8: We Override A Problem With The Word Of God 87
9: Trust Me All The Way. 97

Part Four:

Put Me First **107**

10: The Warfare We Are In Is Real....................... 109

11: Patience Is Very Important To The Lord.............. 119

Part Five:

The Bride Of Christ.................................**133**

12: My Longing For Jesus............................... 135

13: A Humble, Longing, And Expecting Heart 147

Acknowledgments

Never in my whole life could I have imagined writing the acknowledgments for a book I wrote.. I am still in awe of the Lord who enabled me to write and accomplish this.

First of all, I give thanks to my Father in heaven who has chosen me to be His daughter and has also chosen me to belong to His Son, Jesus Christ, as His bride.

I give all my thanks to Jesus who came to redeem me from sin and death and made me whole.

I also thank the Holy Spirit who is at all times my counselor and teacher; without His help I could not have written all the experiences I had with the Lord in book form.

A big thanks to my husband, Henk, who always encouraged me that I could write this book together with the Lord. He stood in faith, and supported me in love when I was stressing and saying, "I don't know how to put this all on paper." Thank you Henk for always telling me that the Lord has called me to write down all the miraculous things He has done for me.

With thanks and gratitude to my daughter, Carla, who has helped me wonderfully with my grammar.

Also a big thanks to Jessica, my granddaughter, who designed the front cover for me so beautifully and entered some of the parts of this book into the computer.

Another big thanks to my son Fred, who helped me out a great deal when I panicked, thinking I had lost my manuscript. I was so thankful that he was able to bring it back again.

Thank you, Gerry, my first born son, and his wife Joanne, for praying for me in times when I needed it.

I also would like to thank my friends for their love and encouragement, which means a lot to me.

Last, but not least, to all the wonderful people at Xulon Press who have helped me patiently with this project.

Introduction

The Bible tells us we are foreordained. It tells us that the Lord knows us and shed His blood for us before we were born, and it tells us about plans to prosper us and not to harm us. The Bible tells us that God loves us even before He reveals it to us. This is almost mind-boggling but so true, and when you read my life story, you will understand why I can fully say amen to this.

Isaiah 61:1 tells us that Jesus was ordained by His Father to preach good news to the lost, to bind up the brokenhearted, heal their wounds, and set the captives free. I am so glad Jesus did this because that's who I was: lost, brokenhearted, wounded, and bound by the enemy.

To write this book was not my idea at all, but it was the Lord's idea. When He made clear to me to put my life story in book form, I was very surprised but also overwhelmed. Me—write a book? How in the world can I do that? My English is not the greatest because it is my second language, so how can I put into words everything I went through? How can I express myself in order for people to be interested to read it all?

I asked the Lord to confirm it to me, and He did this in a way I couldn't get around or explain away. First, through

His Word, in 1 Corinthians 16:9, He said, *"because a great door for effective work has opened to me"* Also, He confirmed it through three different people; one lady, whom I hadn't seen in three years, asked me if I had published my testimony yet. Then a lady from church who had written several books herself asked me if I was interested in writing a book about all the Lord had done in my life. Also, our daughter's friend, who is a pastor, asked me if I would like to write some of my testimonies for her in short form to put it on her website.

That is how I started writing my life story, and I was so glad I had kept up writing for most of my journey through the years. So I started to read those old notebooks to refresh my mind in order to write this book. And believe it or not, I was actually amazed about all the Lord had revealed to me through those years in visions and revelations. It all fitted together so beautifully!

This book is written in five parts because it describes five parts of my life. The first part is about my conversion and the healing and restoration of my soul from the sexual abuse I suffered in my childhood, and how the Lord came to me in that difficult time and blessed me and told me, "At that moment you were Mine."

Three parts are about major attacks on my life and how the Lord warned me of those attacks coming my way though I had no idea what they would be. One time, the Lord told me in a vision to read only scriptures about healing.

Introduction

Months after that vision, I was diagnosed with the most aggressive form of cancer—stage four melanoma. Finally, after weeks of waiting I was able to go through a scan and MRI to determine how much the cancer had spread and what the next step of action would be. In the midst of waiting and reading and meditating on the healing scriptures, the Holy Spirit led me to an amazing scripture that became the title of this book.

There was another attack that came my way where I was at the point of death in my husband's arms, and I became alive again when he spoke over me the words: *"She will not die but live and declare the works of God"* (Psalm 118:17).

Also the Lord revealed the realm of the spirit where we are living in and how to put Him first in my suffering and pain. The Lord taught me the importance of patience that goes along with trusting Him and receiving divine healing. You will read about many visions and revelations the Lord gave me through those years in which He revealed His Word to me in connection with the things I went through. My faith through the years became totally based on the Word of God, and I'm so thankful that those visions were always revealing the reality and the seriousness of the Word. We serve an amazing Lord and Savior who truly cares for us!!!

Years ago, the Lord sent three angels to my bedside after I was diagnosed with an incurable liver disease. And while I was writing this book about the three angels, the Lord told me why there were three angels and not just one (I was always wondering about that).

The last part is about the Bride of Christ and how the Lord showed in a vision that I belong to His bride. That chapter is very precious to me, and when you read it, you will understand why.

Part 1:

How Our Romance —And My Romance With The Lord— Started

Chapter 1

A Prayer, A Dream, A Marriage

In Holland, in a little town, there was a young man who prayed to God and asked the Lord if there was a girl somewhere who was fitting for him. He had spent time with many girls but found no one who was right for him, no one he wanted to share his life with.

In the night, the Lord gave him a dream, and in that dream he saw a girl with blond hair on a bicycle, biking down a country road as she went over a bridge and continued to another town. That's all he saw in that dream, and the Lord said, "She will be your wife." At that moment, he knew in his heart who that blond girl was and where she lived. And he thought, *Somehow I have to make contact with her.* Therefore, on a Sunday night, he went to a social at the church—and yes, there she was, a shy, young girl. That girl was me.

The young man's name was Henk, and he walked up to me and started making conversation with me. After some time, he asked me if I wanted to come with him to a friend's birthday party. I was flabbergasted that he would ask me.

I was already surprised that he had come to talk to me because Henk was very outgoing and popular. I knew him a little because he had been friends with my older brother for a short time. He was very talkative, and I was so shy and insecure and had very low self-esteem, so I could hardly believe he would ask me to come to that friend's birthday party. But I said yes, and that's how we started our dating relationship. He found out quickly, that yes, I was that girl biking on that particular road two times a week.

When Henk told me about that dream, I was even more surprised how God could give him a dream about me. I was raised in a Christian Reformed home, so I knew about dreams and visions from the Bible and how God would speak to people in that way, but a dream or vision about me—that was unthinkable. But, I did love it and felt very special and also thankful.

Before I came into the picture, Henk always went out with friends and led a band. But when we fell in love and were dating, he stopped it all so we could spend more time together. We got married pretty quickly, and my husband was amazing then and still is after fifty years (we just celebrated our fiftieth anniversary). His love for me is unending and deep.

A Drastic Change after Ten Years

After ten years of marriage, our lives changed drastically. One night we went to bed, and after a bit of talking, we held hands and wanted to pray like we always did. But

A Prayer, A Dream, A Marriage

we couldn't pray, and both of us were suddenly, deeply convicted of sin so much that we started to cry. We asked forgiveness of the Lord for our sins, and somehow we knew that we were at a crossroads in our lives. We knew that if we were to continue the way we were living, we would go the wrong way.

We were not in a church service or anything like that. No one was there; we were in bed. We didn't really know what "repentance" meant at that time because that was not preached in our church. We had never heard about being born again either. Praise the Lord; He Himself was intervening in our lives. He was there with His convicting power, and we asked the Lord to forgive us and cleanse us with His blood, saying, "Lord take over our lives, we are going the wrong way. *Take over, Lord. We want to go your way and live with You from now on. Please help us.*"

After that, I started to weep intensely, and finally after ten years of marriage I dared to tell Henk what happened to me when I was a child. I told him that my dad had molested me when I was twelve years old and that I never felt safe or secure when I was home alone with my dad. That was because if he had the chance, he would touch me inappropriately, and that made me fearful my whole childhood. I always felt threatened by him.

Henk reacted so lovingly and said, "Why didn't you tell me that earlier? Now I love you even more." He held me in his arms and comforted me and prayed that the Lord would heal me from all the pain, and, oh my—that felt so good! What comfort and love flooded my soul. I had not told

Henk about it because my dad told me not to tell anyone, and I didn't know how Henk would react because I needed his love so much. Also, I didn't want to hurt Henk by saying how I really felt when we made love and the pain that was there when he poured his love into me. How could I say that his love in that way was hurting me?

No, it was not always that bad, thank God; my husband and I also had good and beautiful times, but it was not easy for me. There always seemed to be a struggle, a battle inside of me, to give myself totally over to Henk, and that had bothered me a lot. *I could not understand why I couldn't give myself to my husband as fully as he did to me.*

I remember that in the first years of my marriage I thought to myself, *How can I handle this for ten years?* There was always that battle inside of me. I didn't know and had no idea that the Lord knew all about my battle. He knew all about my pain, and knew all about my thoughts, my struggles, and frustration about wanting to give myself totally. But I couldn't, and that gave me guilt and doubt of my love for Henk while I loved him so much and admired him for his unconditional love for me.

And then, there it was—after ten years of marriage—that the Lord came to my aid and started to heal the pain inside of me, bit by bit. I will come back to that later on.

Hungry for the Word

From the moment that we gave our lives over to the Lord, we were very hungry to read the Bible and wanted

A Prayer, A Dream, A Marriage

to know all about the Lord who loves us so much. Every spare moment, we picked up our Bible and started to read His wonderful Word. One evening I was reading about Nicodemus where Jesus was telling him, you must be born again in John 3:3-7 *In reply Jesus declared, "I tell you the truth, unless a man is born again, he cannot see the Kingdom of God. How can a man be born when he is old?" Nicodemus asked. "Surely he cannot enter a second time into his mother's womb to be born!" Jesus answered, "I tell you the truth, unless a man is born of water and the Spirit, he cannot enter the Kingdom of God. Flesh gives birth to flesh, but the Spirit gives birth to spirit. You should not be surprised at My saying, you must be born again."* Suddenly the Spirit rose up in me and I shouted to my husband, "Henk, that is what happened to us. We are born again, born by the Spirit of God!"

I was so excited, for that explained perfectly what we were experiencing. We never had heard the words *"you must be born again."* But that is exactly how we felt: like a totally new person and so peaceful inside. It was just as you would see a newborn baby lying so peacefully in his mom's arms. I was also so amazed to know that the Spirit of God was living in us. What an incredible thought that is.

Our friends had already said to us, "What happened to you? You look so happy as if you just came home from your honeymoon." So we told them what had happened. They didn't react in the way that we had hoped they would. They just pushed it away; they didn't really want to hear about our conversion and our love for the Lord Jesus. But they did see the difference in us and that was good to know, and of course, we could feel it too. I even saw it in my face when I looked in the mirror. My eyes were shining as I had never seen before. Finally, I had peace and rest in my heart, which I had never felt before. I was so thankful to my Lord.

Our Journey with the Lord

From that point on, our journey with the Lord started. We have seen Him move and work in many ways in us and in our three children's lives. Many miracles have taken place since then. We have seen instant miracles with our kids when they were sick and also healing over time. The Lord has always been faithful.

One day, my husband was at work and was standing on a ladder to put some screws in a wall. He had to put pressure on those screws, and when he did that, the ladder, which was standing on a slippery tile floor, started to slide. Henk fell straight down onto that tile floor and all the air left his lungs. His face turned blue, and he knew that if no air came back to his lungs he would die. At that point, Henk said, "Lord, I am coming to You, but please take care of Ineke and our children." The moment he said that, the air came back into his lungs and he could breathe again. Praise God, it was not his time to go to heaven yet.

However, he was in terrible pain. His ribs were bruised as well as the heel of his left foot, and he could hardly walk. The man who worked with him wanted to bring him immediately to the hospital or to a doctor, but Henk said, "No, I'm going home. The Lord is my doctor, and He will heal me." He had no choice but to drive Henk home. Henk could hardly walk but made it into the house and told me what had happened. For six weeks he was in a lot of pain, but in the midst of it, he learned to praise the Lord. Praise just rose up out of his spirit, and he glorified the Father in spite of the pain.

Then after six weeks, Henk needed to lift a stack of windows and they were very heavy. He said, "Lord, I need to bring this to my customer. I believe that You have healed me and that You will give me the strength to do this." Instantly, while he was lifting those heavy windows, he was healed. He had absolutely no pain in his back, ribs, or heel anymore. He was totally healed and never had any pain from that tragic moment. Hallelujah—glory to the Lord! This was our first miracle, and many followed after that.

During this time we knew we needed to leave the church we were attending at that time. The Lord guided us to a Full Gospel church, and the first time we were there, during the worship service, someone spoke out a word in combination with a scripture out of Revelation 3:11, saying, "I am coming soon. Hold on to what you have, so that no one will take your crown." When I heard that scripture, it was as if the Lord was speaking directly to me, and my heart was pounding in my chest. That exact scripture was given to me when I did the confession of faith in the church I grew up in. How beautiful that was; the Lord knew all about us and confirmed to us that we were in the right church for that moment.

They were also speaking in tongues, something we had never heard before, and people were stretching out their hands to the Lord in worship. We were not used to any of this, but we loved it, and we were so hungry for all the things of the Lord. People were very friendly to us. Rightaway the first time we were in that church someone invited us for coffee, and it so happened that they were having a birthday party. Because of it we met many of the people from the church, and we were able to make great contacts that first Sunday.

Baptism in Water

After some time, we discovered that water baptism means a person was to be immersed in water, not just being sprinkled with water. We wanted to obey the Lord and His Word and be baptized the correct way. It was a while before we were able to be baptized because they just had a baptismal service.

But when the day arrived, it was wonderful. During the baptismal service, there were seven different people who had a word for us; this was very special to us. All those words we have seen as true in our lives throughout the years. Also, we were baptized in the Spirit and spoke in tongues, and since then we have experienced the gifts of the Spirit operating in and through us.

At that time our children were twelve, nine, and five years old, and they too gave their hearts to the Lord. When we laid our hands on them, they also started speaking in tongues. Fred, our youngest, said, "*I only got one word.*" But we encouraged him to speak that one word and told him that the Lord would give him more words, to just speak out what he was given. And soon after, the Lord gave him more words. How precious is that! Yes, it was so precious seeing our own children giving their lives to the Lord and speaking in tongues. They now have their own families, and all of our ten grandchildren are following the Lord. Praise the Lord for His abundance of grace.

The Healing of My Wounded Soul

When the Lord started to heal my soul, I wasn't even aware of how wounded I was until the Lord showed it to my husband. Henk asked the Lord; how can I pray and how can I help my wife, show me what is going on in her soul. He asked this because many times he felt my pain and realized that I didn't know how to express my feelings. The Lord is so good and answered Henk's prayer. He showed Henk a big wound with black, clotted blood. The wound was closed up with five big iron clamps. Over time, and one by one, those five iron clamps came out through deliverance and healing.

Many times when we had gone to bed and we were just talking about things or praying, the Lord would help and heal me. I would start crying. One night, the Lord gave Henk insight into what was going on in my soul and gave him the words to pray and the wisdom on how to deal with it. When Henk was praying for me and spoke my name, something was triggered in me. At that moment, I felt a lot of resistance in me against my name. I could hardly stand hearing it, and I could not even speak out my own name. I hated my name. I hated the name Ineke because I hated myself. And when I realized and understood that, I started to pray about it, and at that moment the Lord gave me a vision.

In that vision, I saw myself standing on a mountain. I threw an old, brown bag off that mountain, and the Lord impressed on me that I had thrown myself away like that old, brown bag. I found myself worthless, and I knew I had to confess that to the Lord before He could heal and change my thinking so I could accept myself for who I was. I knew I sinned against God who created me because His Word says in Psalm 139:13–14, *"For You created my inmost being, You knit me together in my mother's womb. I praise You because I am fearfully and wonderfully made, Your works are wonderful, I know that full well."* When I realized that God Himself had made me, I understood that He also wanted me or He would not have created me. That Psalm says He made me fearfully and wonderfully, and God only creates good things. And yes, what He has created, He also loves.

Then suddenly it dawned on me and I knew in my heart that God loved me. Yes, He loved *me*! At that moment, I realized I didn't even have the right to reject myself.

I confessed my sin of rejecting and hating myself, and Henk prayed for me and spoke against that spirit of rejection. Thank God, I was delivered from that terrible spirit.

A Prayer, A Dream, A Marriage

That spirit of rejection came in because of the circumstances I grew up in. I felt worthless. I always felt stepped on, just as you would step on an insect to kill it. I didn't know why, but that was how I felt.

Rejection is evil, and it hurts terribly, and because of it, my soul was deeply wounded. Rejection is a big weapon of the enemy, and he uses it wherever he can to separate people from each other and to destroy marriages, families, and relationships. Like John 10:10 says; *"The thief comes only to steal and kill and destroy; I have come that you may have a life, and have it to the full."* Thank you Jesus that You came to give us life to the full!!!

When I was delivered and healed from that rejection, I felt so much better. I knew my husband loved me, but for the first time, I *felt* that I was loved. I could receive his love in my heart and did not reject it anymore. Before that, I longed for his love, but because of what was in me, I could not fully receive and accept his love which I needed so desperately.

Thank God that when we cry out to the Lord, He doesn't leave us alone, but is full of compassion over us and lifts us up and heals us through His mighty love. Jesus says in His Word in Matthew 11:28 *"Come to Me, all you who are weary and burdened and I will give you rest."* Jesus is the one who gives us rest and peace. He is the healer of all our wounds and pains, and He is the one who helps us and gives us the strength to go on in life. And I tell you, I needed that strength to keep going.

Chapter 2

Confrontation With My Dad

I needed that strength from the Lord very much because, after a while, the Lord impressed on me very strongly that I had to confront my dad with what he had done to me. This was very difficult for me to do. I prayed a lot about it and asked the Lord if I really had to do this because I thought it would certainly break my mom's heart when she heard about it. How could I tell my mom? She knew nothing about it. I never told her nor anyone else besides my husband. After some time, the Lord gave me a vision and, in that vision; I had a cup and saucer in my hands. On the top of the cup was a heavy pressure, and I was holding that cup up in order that the saucer would not break under that pressure.

The Lord said, "When you go to your parents and open up about what happened to you, I can bring your mom into a place to save her soul. In a sense, she needs to be broken. She has to come to Me and cry out to Me to be saved."

I said, "Okay, Lord, I will do anything for my mom to be saved, but, Lord, You have to help me. I need You so much in this. I don't want to hurt my mom, not even my dad, by bringing this up after all these years."

So my husband and I went to their home one night. Unexpectedly, my mom was not at home. The Lord had worked it out beautifully so that we could first talk to my dad without my mom. It was not easy to confront him with his hurtful and inappropriate behavior, He even denied it and said, "I don't remember that anymore; that was such a long time ago." When my mom came home, she was very surprised to see us. Because we were living an hour away from them, we always called ahead and made sure they were home before we visited. We soon told her the reason why we had come by and about all that had happened in the past. She was shocked and saddened because she had no idea that this had been happening in her house.

She never shed a tear during the time we were there, but she broke down at night. It was very hard for her to deal with the reality of what had happened, and, of course, I understood that fully. It took her a long time before she really gave her life to Jesus, but she did, and it is wonderful to know that she is saved and with the Lord. She is safe in the arms of Jesus with no pain in her heart anymore, finally free from all the tension she lived within her married life.

What Had Happened When I Was a Little Child

I always knew what my dad had done to me when I was twelve years old, but in my heart, I felt there was more.

Confrontation With My Dad

Had something else happened to me when I was just a little child? For some time, in my spirit, I had been seeing myself as a little child, lying in the woods somewhere, with the feeling of ants creeping over my body, with a man beside me. That's all I knew. I didn't know if it really happened or if it was a dream/nightmare. But I couldn't get rid of it, so I started to pray and ask the Lord to show me what this was all about.

At the time, we had a plant hanging in our kitchen window, and for a couple of days, I had been seeing fine soil laying on the window ledge under that plant. I thought, *"This looks like fine soil that you see in a garden when there are ants in the soil.*" For a few days I cleaned it up every morning, but one morning, I wanted to see what was going on with that plant. I took it off the hook and walked with it to the backyard. I took the plant out of the pot, and there I saw a nest with ants, lots of them, as well as little white eggs. The moment I saw those ants, something inside of me triggered. I threw the plant on the grass, ran into the house, and went upstairs to my bedroom. I fell face down on our bed and cried my heart out. I was sobbing so loudly and was glad that the children were at school. I was by myself, just me and the Lord.

At that moment, I understood the vision I had in my heart. That man beside me in the woods was real, and that had really happened to me. Laying on the bed, I could feel the pain and even the ants crawling over my body. I wept for a long time, and healing took place in my soul. But there was much more healing to come. I was so impressed by the Lord, that He revealed the truth unto me in such an amazing way. He somehow brought a nest of ants in a plant hanging in my kitchen window and that bit of soil that had drawn my attention to examine that plant.

When I was getting to the mystery of the dirt and that plant, not a hair on my head was thinking about the connection with that vision, of seeing myself lying in the woods on a nest of ants. But the Lord knew. He already prepared that nest with ants to answer my prayer. *God is so good and worthy to be praised!*

Four Years Old

After a month or so, the Lord put in my memory what my mom told me about something that had happened when I was four years old. I was crying throughout the night and she kept on asking me why I was crying, but I didn't say anything. The only thing I did was hold both of my little hands over my lower stomach and cry. The next morning, my mom brought me to the doctor to find out what was wrong with my stomach. Because I didn't say anything, they examined me and tried to see what was wrong. The doctor thought that my appendix might be bursting. So in a hurry, they brought me to the hospital for an operation to take my appendix out. But when they opened it up, there was nothing wrong with my appendix, but the surgeon took it out anyway.

When I was thinking and praying about this event, I suddenly knew and understood what had happened in the

Confrontation With My Dad

woods that day, and why I cried the whole night, and also why I had held my hands on my lower stomach. I was probably in such shock at what had happened to me that day so that I couldn't say anything or explain anything about it. How can you explain this when you are only four years old? Now I understand the shock and the trauma that had such a great effect on me growing up.

It was always difficult for me to talk freely and express myself. I was insecure and very shy when I was with people. I didn't know what to say, so I was very quiet. My mom told me once that when I was little, we were at my aunt's on a Sunday afternoon, and when it was time to go home, they didn't know where I was. They couldn't find me, and when they called my name, I came from behind the couch where I was hiding. That's how shy I was.

When I came to the Lord and got to know Him better and was growing in my faith, the Lord liberated me bit by bit through the healing of my soul. Hallelujah, I'm so thankful! Now I'm outgoing and able to reach out and talk to people. I love to encourage and pray for people, even if it is in a store it doesn't bother me at all. *I am a totally new person, and my identity is in Christ.* I'm now the offspring from my heavenly Father, not of my earthly father anymore. I am born again, born of God. Glory forever to my heavenly Father.

We Immigrated to Canada

Now I'd like to go on with my story. Up to this point, my husband and I were living in Holland, but we felt it was God's plan to immigrate to Canada. My two brothers had been living in Canada for years already, and they helped us immigrate. For the first nine years of our marriage, we owned a greenhouse business that we sold and then moved to another part of Holland. It was there that we came to know the Lord.

For the first two years of living in Canada, my husband worked for a greenhouse business, but at the same time we also started a flower business of our own again, just as we had in Holland. Besides our house, we had a piece of land. We sowed flower seeds and started to grow flowers. When they were ready to be sold, we cut them in the evenings when Henk was home, and during the day I made bunches of the flowers in order to sell them to wholesalers. The selling of the flowers was new for me; I had never been in sales before. In order to start, I had to find wholesalers to sell my product. Not knowing any wholesalers and having to approach them in my broken English, I had to overcome my fear. But thank God, most of them were Dutch, so they understood my dilemma. They were very nice to me, and I was able to sell our flowers.

One day when I was bunching flowers, I was listening to a tape from a woman who shared a part of her testimony. As I listened to her, I suddenly began to cry deep from my belly, and I wasn't sure what the reason for this was. Because

Confrontation With My Dad

I was working, I could not give it my full attention, and I wasn't able to hear everything the lady was saying. So I said to the Lord, "What is this about?" I rewound the cassette tape back partly and listened to it again; now it had my full attention.

Something had happened to that lady when she was four years of age, something that was devastating to her. Something that was most precious to her was suddenly taken out of her life. When I heard what she related, I wept again and knew that this was from the deep wound in my soul from when I was four years old. It was hurting again so much; it was so deep. I can't explain it, but I listened to that part of the tape over and over again and, through that process, the Lord continued healing me from all that inner pain. I sobbed until it didn't hurt anymore.

This was the deepest wound, the deepest pain I had experienced in my life. I knew in my heart that this was about what had happened in the woods with that man. Now years later, reading the notes about this again to refresh my memory and to be able to write it all down, the Lord started to reveal to me what really happened there in the woods, things I didn't know before. *It was shocking to me.*

The Lord said that my virginity was taken away from me, the most precious part of women, and He also said it was too difficult for a four-year-old child to comprehend all this. With my mind, I knew that my virginity was taken away in the natural, but I had no idea that this was also a spiritual matter that caused such a deep wound in my soul.

We as human beings think so lightly about these things because we think it is only in the natural. *But for God, it is of great importance because it is a spiritual matter.*

The Last Piece of the Puzzle

The last piece of this puzzle for me was, who was this man who was with me in the woods? I asked the Lord, "I know You know who this man was; was this my dad or someone else?" I didn't want to believe it was my dad, and I didn't want to know if it was so. To know that it was my father was too painful for me to accept. But in my heart, I was almost certain that it was him. *I pushed it away for a long time until I was ready for it. And the Lord knew exactly that time.*

On a Sunday morning, when I was having my devotion with the Lord, I was suddenly certain in my heart that it was my dad, and finally I could accept this and had peace about it. It was strange but true. The Lord had perfect timing. It was still difficult for me to comprehend that a father could do this to his own child, but I also knew that he was driven by the enemy. The enemy doesn't care who it is. The enemy's only purpose is to steal, kill, and destroy. But, praise Jesus, He came to give me life and has healed me through all His loving care and kindness to me.

I am so thankful for all the healing in my soul; it has made me free and happy. I remember when I was a child that I was jealous of the girls at school that they could laugh from deep within and I could not. At that time I didn't understand why, but now I know that the trauma had locked me up till the Lord healed and delivered me from it. Now I have joy and can laugh from my heart and thank God for it!!! Now I can praise God out of my innermost being, now I know that God is good and loves me deeply, something I could never comprehend before.

In the End, It Is Worth Every Tear

I'm finding most people bury their pain and don't want to talk about it or deal with it, especially such things as I went through, because it hurts too much. Some other people like to just talk about the hurt all the time, and by doing so, they pamper it with self-pity and that is not good either. And yes, I know it hurts terribly when you go through the process of healing. *But it is worth every tear for the freedom and joy you receive through it at the end.*

From the beginning I prayed about the whole process of healing and told the Lord that I really wanted to be healed from all the abuse that had wounded my soul. I wanted to be whole so that I could enjoy my husband and love him with all my heart, to make him happy, and of course, so that I could enjoy my love life too. Now we can have pleasure together which I couldn't have dreamed of before.

I gave the Lord the lead, and He made everything beautiful in His time. All came forth at the right time when I was ready for it. But at times I said, "Lord, is there still more? I thought that I was done with it." Then I found out that healing most of the time comes gradually. I know if all the work of healing was done at once, I could not have endured it. Again, the Lord knows what we can handle and what we cannot. He is so good. There was also healing and cleansing of several things of which I had no idea, things I never even felt bothered by. But the Lord knew all about it and brought it forth in His time, and in such a way that only the Lord can do.

In Awe of the Lord

Truly, I'm in awe of the Lord every time when He does something out of the blue. The next story was such an experience. One very cold night in April, we went with a group from our church to Toronto to minister to homeless people. There were people lying on the sidewalk, people sitting with blankets over them or wearing double jackets. There was also a couple with a small child, and it was heartbreaking to see such a small child on the street in the cold. We talked to those people, told them about the Lord, and showed His love and care for them by giving them sandwiches, apples, or bananas. We also gave them socks. They liked the socks the best; that was a great treat for them. It was so sad to hear some of their stories and how some of them ended up on the street like that.

One man was laying on a piece of cardboard on the sidewalk, and the cardboard was placed on a register where the heat came through. It seemed like he was sound asleep, and we didn't want to bother him by waking him up for a talk. So we just put some sandwiches and socks under his blanket.

Confrontation With My Dad

At that moment, he awoke and got up to see what was going on. He lifted his blanket and by doing so, an awful smell came up from under it. The smell struck me so heavily, but it didn't bother my husband at all. When we heard the man speak, it was unbelievable.

He spoke with several different voices. It was as if there were different persons in this man who were talking to us. And through the things he told us, we sensed those were demons speaking through that man. Henk talked with him for a while. The sad thing was that he was not open to the Lord at all, but he was thankful for the sandwiches and socks. Hopefully, he will remember the words Henk spoke to him.

That was our last visit for the night, and from there we went to Tim Hortons to meet our group and went home. When we were home after an hour of driving in a warm van, we were still cold and said to each other, "How in the world can those people handle this cold weather and be on the street day and night in these cold temperatures?" The only thing we wanted to do when we got home was go to bed and get warm. Even in our comfortable bed, it took us a while before we got warm again. During getting warm, my husband did something he never had done before; it was something my dad did to me once. At that moment I felt so used, so awfully dirty like that dirty smell that came from under the blanket of that homeless man in Toronto.

I started to cry and told Henk what my dad had done and how I was feeling at that moment. I told him that I felt so dirty, like that smell of the homeless man, and also that

I felt so used. I cried and cried for a long time, and deep healing took place in my soul while Henk prayed for me. In the meantime, Henk felt bad about what he did and was very sorry. But I said, "You could not know this, Henk, so don't feel bad at all or worry about it. The Lord has brought this whole situation of going to Toronto and meeting this homeless man in our lives right now to heal me from this deep wound and cleanse me from it."

I was very thankful to my Lord, my Healer, and my Deliverer. This was the last clamp that came out of the wound, as Henk had seen in that vision some time before. It was the last of the five iron clamps that were holding that big wound together, with all the black, clotted blood. Now I was healed from all that pain, and I am so grateful to my Lord who made me free. I am free to love my heavenly Father and free to love my husband with all the love the Lord has bestowed upon me.

Chapter 3

Forgiveness Brings Us Into Victory

One point I haven't touched on yet is forgiveness. It is extremely important in the process of inner healing for those of us who are victims of abuse of any kind. Our forgiveness brings us out of the state of being victims and brings us into victory. Yes, it conquers over the past and over the situation we are in. Forgiveness is a principle in the Bible we have to live by. I realize many of you may be in a very tough and painful situation at the moment and have suffered even more than I have. And, yes, it looks hopeless to you in the natural, but with our God, nothing is impossible. With God, there are no impossibilities. He can rescue us out of every pit, out of all the darkness and pain we are in.

Jesus is always our example. When He was suffering so much and dying on the cross, Jesus forgave all they had done to Him and said, *"Father, forgive them, for they do not know what they are doing"* (Luke 23:34).

And in Colossians 3:13 it says, *"Forgive whatever grievances you may have against one another."* Even after that, it says very plainly and boldly: *"Forgive as the Lord forgave you."*

Plainly and boldly is the best way to forgive. I found out that the best way to do this is to make a decision in your heart to forgive. And after that, say it out loud and boldly: **"I forgive as my Lord Jesus forgave me."**

If we wait to forgive until our feelings line up with it, it may never come. But if we decide in our hearts to forgive with our understanding, the Lord will be right there to help us forgive the one who has hurt us because it is His will that we forgive. If we put our will into forgiving the other person, our feelings will fall in line with our decision. When we are hurting so deeply, we usually will have to do this more than once. But we have to stand firm because the enemy will haunt us with it and will say, "You didn't really forgive with your heart because look at you, it is still hurting you a lot." *Slam it back in his face and tell Satan, "Get behind me; I did forgive as the Lord Jesus forgave me."*

I have experienced this over and over, and the Lord helped me to forgive my dad bit by bit. I had to do it over and over again, but I decided to forgive from my heart because I wanted to make sure that my heart was pure before my Lord.

A Clean Heart to Love My Dad with All My Heart

I remember the time that my mom and dad came from Holland to visit my two brothers and us. Before they came, I asked the Lord to let me experience and know that my heart was totally clean so I could love my dad with my whole heart, without any resistance. When they came over, believe it or not, my heart went out to my father, and I was glad to see him. I hugged him with love and compassion. That love continued throughout the time they were here with us, and it also stayed with me until he passed away some years later. To think that a couple of years prior to the moment of their visit with us, I felt so much hatred towards him.

One Sunday driving back from church, my husband said something to me, and I felt such irritation and resentment in my heart toward him. This resentment and irritation was happening quite frequently. And every time I would ask forgiveness from the Lord because I knew it wasn't right, and I didn't want that feeling in my heart. When we got home, I went to my husband in the living room where he was reading a book, and I actually knelt before him, told him how I was feeling, and asked for forgiveness. While I was doing that, I noticed the picture of my dad behind him there on a shelf. At that moment, I felt so much hatred in my heart toward my dad that I could have almost punched him in his face. I never felt such hatred against my dad before, and at that moment, I suddenly knew what was going on in me. I realized that the resentment and irritation toward my husband had its roots in the hatred I felt in my heart against my dad.

Right away I said, "Lord forgive me. Forgive me that I hated my dad. I don't want to have that in my heart, not one moment longer." I told my husband what was going on inside of me and how I felt. I also asked my husband to forgive me and the Lord delivered me the moment he prayed for me. Thank God for the cleansing blood of Jesus!!!

I wondered why that hatred had never shown up before that moment. I never felt hatred toward my dad; this was the first time after all those years. Then the Lord showed me that I had pushed that hatred so deep down in my heart that it couldn't come to the surface. I knew it was wrong to hate my father, and I didn't know how to deal with it, so I just didn't allow hatred to show up in my heart and didn't even want to think about it. *But I thank God that He brought it to my attention, in order to be freed from this hatred and be cleansed at the same time.*

My Husband Felt My Pain Many Times

The Lord used my husband many times in the healing and forgiving process. He knew the pain I had been in because, many times, the Lord let him feel the pain I was feeling when I couldn't express what was going on inside of me and the only thing I could do was cry. In those moments, the Lord revealed to him the things that were battering me, or Henk just spoke about things that triggered something inside of me, and at that moment, I was aware and understood why I was crying.

I believe the reason the Lord let Henk feel my pain was so that he could pray for me effectively. Because he felt my pain, Henk's heart was involved, and he could pray with compassion for me and could minister to me through the amazing love of Jesus. *Several times it happened that Henk felt and experienced the love of God pouring into his heart, and then he felt that love flowing out of him and into my heart.*

How wonderful and mighty our Lord is, that He is able to do things like fill us with His love, and heal and comfort us with His love!

One time, the Lord said to my husband, "Ineke is crushed inside." Who can be healed from being crushed deep in their soul other than through our Lord Jesus? Many people go for treatments for years, and many times they are still not healed. Things will go okay for a while, but when something happens that reminds them of the past and it triggers the pain of what was still there, and they are back to where they started. And because of it, they get so discouraged, and many times depression follows.

No one except our Lord Jesus can restore and heal our souls because He Himself *"was pierced for our transgressions, He was crushed for our iniquities, the punishment that brought us peace was upon Him, and by His wounds, we are healed* (Isa. 53:5). In the Amplified version, it also says *"by His wounds we are healed and made whole."*

The Lord knows and has felt what it means to be crushed, not only in His body but also deep in His soul. He was crushed for our iniquities, yes, but also *He bore our soul pain in order to heal us from it.* Everything the Lord suffered on the cross was for us. This is what's called the exchange on the cross. All the bad things that were our fault came upon Jesus, and in exchange, all the good that Jesus brought forth was given to us. He has felt your and my soul pain, our pain, which is sometimes even too deep to express in words. His wounds and pain are far over and above anything we can ever imagine.

Jesus, the only Son of God, came to this earth to save us, to heal us from our brokenness, and to do us good. But over and over, Jesus experienced rejection by His own people whom He came to save because He loved them. *Jesus felt the pain of not being accepted and pushed away.* In Nazareth where He grew up, they even wanted to push Him off a cliff. They want to get rid of Him and kill Him. At another time, they wanted to stone Him. Jesus was disowned by one of His friends. He was betrayed by one of His disciples.

Through all of this, you can see how much and how deeply Jesus suffered in His pure and undefiled soul.

We can't even think of or imagine how much Jesus suffered. Think of all the pressure that came upon His soul in Gethsemane. And, how about the whipping post and the cross?

For Jesus to know that He would be made sin with all our sin and rebellion and that He was to be separated from His Father would seem to be unbearable for Him. It says in Mark 14:33–34 that Jesus was deeply distressed and troubled, His soul was overwhelmed with sorrow even to the point of death. His soul was under so much stress and sorrow that He almost died there, and in Luke 22:44, it says His sweat was like drops of blood falling to the ground. Sweat turning to drops of blood can only happen under a tremendous amount of pressure. *Jesus bore all our soul pain so that we can be healed. He felt that pain in His own soul in all the ways we have been wounded.* When we cry out to

Him for healing in our soul, He still feels it. His heart is full of compassion, and He reaches out to us with deep love to heal us completely.

The Pain of Betrayal

The Lord also knew that I needed to be restored from having been betrayed by my dad, even though I wasn't even aware of it. I knew my trust was broken, but I never looked at it as being betrayed as well. One morning, when I was reading my Bible, I read in 1 Corinthians 11:23 that the Lord was betrayed by Judas. As I was reading this, I suddenly started to cry deep from within my soul. At that moment, I felt the pain of being betrayed by my dad, something I had never felt before. At the moment of weeping, the Lord healed me in part. A month or two later, the same thing happened to me by reading that same scripture. At that point, the healing was complete.

I don't know the reason why this happened two separate times. But I do know that a betrayal from someone close to us results in deep wounding of our souls. That is probably the reason why. Thank you, Jesus, for carrying that for us also.

The Warning in the Bible about Not Forgiving One Another Is Clear

There is another reason why we need to forgive. The Bible is very clear in this, and we had better listen to be wise to put God's words in to practice in order to stand against the storms of life. To have our feet on the Rock as Jesus told us in Matthew 7:24-27, so that we don't fall. There is a strong caution for us in Matthew 6. In verse 12, the Lord tells us in the Lord's prayer that we forgive our debtors. In the Amplified version, it also says: "let go of resentment against our debtors." Then Jesus continues in verse 14: *"For if you forgive men when they sin against you, your heavenly Father will also forgive you. But if you do not forgive men their sins, your Father will not forgive your sins."*

We have to forgive and show mercy like our Father in heaven does, as it is stated in Luke 6:36: *"Be merciful, just as your Father is merciful."*

In Matthew 18:21–22, Peter asked Jesus a great question: *"Lord, how many times shall I forgive my brother when he sins against me? Up to seven times?" Jesus answered: "I tell you, not seven times but seventy-seven times."* Right after this, Jesus tells them of the parable of the unmerciful servant in verses 23–35. He said:

> The Kingdom of heaven is like a king who wanted to settle accounts with his servants. One owed him a great amount of money and because he couldn't pay, he fell on his knees and begged him to be patient with him. And the king took pity on him and canceled all his debt and let him go free. Then this same servant found one of his fellow servants who owed him just a little,

he grabbed him and demanded him to pay back what he owed him. This fellow servant fell on his knees also, and begged him to be patient until he could pay him back.

But he refused to give him mercy as he received mercy just a short time before. Instead, he had the man thrown into prison until he could pay the debt.

And when the king heard it, he called the servant back and said to him: 'You wicked servant, I canceled all that debt of yours because you begged me to. Shouldn't you have had mercy on your fellow servant just as I had on you?'

In anger, he turned him over to the jailers (this means torturers) until he could pay back all he owed.

Now we see in verse 35 how earnest the Word of God is. It says, *"This is how my heavenly Father will treat each of you unless you forgive your brother from your heart."* Forgiveness plays a big role in our healing. Jesus plainly tells us that if we don't forgive as He has forgiven us, the Father won't forgive us and will give us over to the jailers, the tormentors. No one wants that to happen in their lives, but in reality, we see this all around us. Many people are spiritually bound up. Many are living in depression and get easily angered over little things. Even some doctors will tell you that many illnesses are a direct result of anger, hate, and unforgiveness.

In order to be wise and build our house on a sure foundation, we need to take the Word very seriously, so we can enjoy life and be free in the spirit. We need to love and have compassion for each other, and even do good to our enemies. As it says in Luke 6:35–36: *"Then your reward will be great, and you will be sons of the Highest. Because He is kind to the ungrateful and the wicket. Be merciful, just as your Father is merciful."*

What I always say to myself is this: I want to show off who my Father in heaven is—kind, loving, forgiving, and joyful. Yes, I want the fruit of the Spirit to show up in my life and honor the Father of glory through it.

You know, God is getting the blame for so many things. When something goes wrong, many people blame God for it right away instead of thinking: *Who is the author of all those bad things?* It isn't God. He is the author of all the good in our lives, Jesus said in John 10:10: *"The thief (Satan) comes only to steal and kill and destroy; I have come that they may have life and have it to the full."*

Through the knowledge of the Word of God, we get discernment and open eyes to see where the enemy tries to come in and pollute our thinking.

The enemy wants to condemn us by saying that what happened is all your fault. And then, on top of that, he wants us to believe that God is punishing us for it. No! God will never punish you if you got abused as a child. Neither is it ever your fault! The devil always wants to condemn us so that we will feel guilty and get down and depressed. When we feel guilty and down, we will not go freely to the Lord and that is where the devil is after, yes to hold us back from the Lord wherever he can. The Lord never ever condemns us or makes us feel guilty or punishes us. No! He will restore us in His love when we come to Him. He always has His heart and arms wide open to us. He loves us with tenderness and compassion, and wants to heal and restore us so that we can be whole again.

Jesus is the one who gives us life to the fullest. Jesus is a life-giving Spirit; that life is always flowing out of Him to us when we cry out and open our hearts for Him.

There are times we believe the lies of the enemy and blame God, just as in my situation. What could I do as a four-year-old against my dad's actions? I trusted and loved my dad. And even when I was twelve and was overpowered by him, that was not my fault. I had to ask for forgiveness from the Lord for blaming Him. It was not the Lord but the devil behind all this. He came to steal, kill, and destroy me. First of all, he stole my trust, my security, my virginity, secondly my innocence, and my purity of heart. And thirdly, he also stole my happiness. He destroyed it all. That is why it took so long to be totally restored back to the way the Lord had created me. The Lord restored me to be the woman He originally planned me to be, to function and to be able to trust my husband and give myself to him.

The Lord also wants us to be like little children, to live free in joy and peace, and trust in God, and to have faith as

We Are Trophies Of Christ's Victory

a child. Years ago, the Lord gave me a picture. I saw myself sitting on my father's lap as a little child, (before I was molested) relaxed with no fear, looking up to him with love and an open face. As I remembered this, right away I said, "Lord, I want to be like this picture again looking up to You, as my heavenly Father, with an open face, no shame or fear, but with joy in my heart and eyes full of expectation." Yes, I wanted to be the way I was before, innocent, pure, harmless, free from destructive sin, and open and joyful. I also said to the Lord, "Father, from now on, I want to trust You fully and honor You as my Father, pleasing You and being a blessing unto You in everything I do."

Chapter 4

Our Lord Is Omnipotent

I found in an old notebook where the Lord told me and showed me things that are very personal and precious to me. Actually, I was hesitating and not sure if I could share this with you, but the Lord made it clear to me that I should write this down because He said, "Many have the same questions you had, and they will be blessed to receive answers through this." Here it is. I asked the Lord about the things that had happened to me when I was so young. I couldn't understand why all this had happened to me.

I didn't ask those questions out of anger or bitterness, but I just wanted some answers from the Lord. And He answered me in a way that surprised me. To be honest with you, at first I could hardly believe that it was the Lord who showed and told me this. I was astonished by what He revealed to me. I asked the Lord, "Where were You when I was raped when I was only four years old? The Bible says You are omnipotent, so where were you?" After asking this question, I saw in the spirit the Lord standing with His hands lifted, and glory came like a ray from His hands toward me.

Then I asked: "Lord, why were you standing with Your hands stretched out and blessing me with your glory while I was laying there with my dad?"

The Lord said, *"My heart went out to you, and I was loving you, and at that moment you were mine!"*

The next question was: "Lord, where were You when I was twelve?" At that moment, I saw the Lord sitting beside me on the bed with his hand on my head, and I felt peace flowing into my heart. I also asked the Lord. "Why, Lord, did You let it happen to me?

The Lord responded to me by saying, "I could do nothing. I couldn't go against the evil desires of your dad. Adam gave himself to Satan, and now Satan and mankind are ruling this earth." Surprisingly the Lord also said, "I have given sex for pleasure between husband and wife, *not* to harm you! My heart always goes out to the brokenhearted. I came to this world to save the lost and set the captives free."

This conversation was astounding to me and still is! I'm so thankful that He revealed those things to me and to know that He has chosen me. The God of all ages came to me when I was so vulnerable, was molested, and couldn't defend myself. He had chosen me. I was so overwhelmed by knowing that He chose me. I know that's what the Bible says, but to hear the Lord saying it and seeing this all in the spirit, touched me deeply.

This is for all of us! It is Jesus who gave His life for us, who sacrificed Himself for us in order to save us. *It is God who has chosen us, not we ourselves.* Thank you, Jesus, for your saving grace!!!

Jesus Is Close to Those Who Are Broken and Crushed

I absolutely love it when I find the same scriptures in different places in the Bible and can personally relate to them. The scripture of Isaiah 61 is also in Psalm 34:18, and it tells us that the Lord is close to the brokenhearted. I'm so thankful the Lord is close to us who are brokenhearted and wants to save those who are crushed in spirit. How true that is! I always felt stepped on and crushed, as someone would step on an insect and turn their foot on it to kill that insect.

In Acts 10:38 it says that God anointed Jesus of Nazareth with the Holy Spirit and power, and that He went around doing good and healing all who were under the power of the devil because God was with Him. In the Dutch Bible, it says, "healing all who were overpowered by the devil." That is what happened to me and many of you. We were overpowered by the enemy, but Jesus came to heal us and set us free. Hallelujah, glory to God! First John 3:8 says, *"The reason the Son of God appeared was to destroy the works of the devil."*

Another time I asked the Lord about the times when I would work with my dad in the barn, grading tomatoes, feeling so afraid and threatened, but nothing happened to me. After my pondering, I saw in the Spirit the Lord sitting at my feet. It was astounding for me to see this. He came to me as my servant sitting at my feet. At this time, I understood that the Lord had protected me for more harm.

The Lord is beyond our imagination. He is incredible. Jesus came to this earth as our servant. He humbled Himself and became like us to serve us. Listen to what it says in Philippians 2:5–7: *"Your attitude should be the same as that of Christ Jesus. Who being in very nature God, did not consider equality with God something to be grasped, but made Himself nothing, taking the very nature of a servant, being made in human likeness."*

In this Scripture, we see clearly that Jesus, in very nature God, let go of all the privileges and rightful dignity, as it says in the Amplified Bible, and came to serve us. He was obedient to His Father and humbled Himself to the extreme of death, even the death of the cross. Jesus didn't do it for Himself; no, He served us and showed through the cross the full extent of His love as it is stated in John 13:1. And then in verses 4–17, the Lord tells us how we should be humble in practical ways, like the washing of His disciples' feet.

When Jesus had finished washing the feet of the disciples, He asked them:

> *Do you understand what I have done for you? You call Me Teacher and Lord and rightly so, for that is what I am. Now that I, your Lord and Teacher, have washed your feet, you also should wash one another's feet. I have set you an example that you should*

*do as I have done for you. I tell you the truth,
no servant is greater than his master, and
no one who is sent is superior to the one who
sent him. Now that you know these things
you will be blessed if you do them.*

Through the humility of Jesus and His total obedience to the Father, God exalted Him to the highest place and gave Him the name that is above every name (see Philippians 2:9). Jesus is our example. When we live in humility and obedience, and die to ourselves as Jesus did, God the Father will exalt us and make us into the bride of Christ.

That is what Paul meant in Philippians 3:14 (Amp) when he said: "*I press on toward the goal to win the supreme and heavenly prize to which God in Christ Jesus is calling us upward.*" The supreme and heavenly calling of God is, first of all, to be saved, to be with God forever, but secondly to be the bride of Jesus. There is no higher place than being the bride of the Son of God. This is why the requirements are so high—to live a holy and pure life before God. In 2 Corinthians 11:2 (AMP), Paul, through the Spirit says: "*For I am zealous for you with a godly eagerness and a divine jealousy, for I have betrothed you to one Husband, to present you as a pure virgin to Christ.*" I am in awe of the Lord to know that He has chosen us to be His bride forever.

Author's Note and Prayer

This was my story, but I realize every one of you has a story to tell. When we all look back into our lives, we see God's hand in guiding and helping us. At times, when everything goes well, we shout, "Glory," but in our difficult times we cry out, "Help." And in those hard and painful times, it is not always easy to see God's hand working, or sometimes we don't even expect His help. But God is faithful and true; He will help us to the very end!!!

> *My Lord, I am so thankful for your faithfulness and that I can come freely and in boldness to your throne of grace to pray for your people. And in Jesus' name, I pray for your grace to come upon families, moms and dads, children and grandparents, to overflow them with your love and grant them your deliverance and healing in any and every way they are in need of right now.*
>
> *Lord, I pray for those who feel that they are ripped apart through separation or molestation. Lord, release your mighty strength and pour out your healing power upon them and let your beloved children experience in their hearts the reality of your love and goodness.*

Our Lord Is Omnipotent

Also, Lord, I ask You to send ministering angels out to them in their time of need because You know exactly what is needed in every person's life.

I thank and praise You for answering my prayer in Jesus' name, amen.

Part 2:

We Are Trophies Of Christ's Victory

Chapter 5

A Warning Through A Vision

"He sent forth His Word and healed them, and delivered them from destruction" (Psalm 107:20).

In February 2012, the Lord gave me a vision; I saw myself sitting in my chair reading my Bible when, suddenly, it became pitch dark, and I felt the house shaking like an earthquake. I heard the Lord saying: "Read every scripture about healing. Forget all the others; read only scriptures about healing." And again I heard: "Read only the scriptures about healing."

I thought, *Oh Lord, what is going on, I am healthy*. But I knew in my heart that this was very serious and that the Lord was warning me of something to come. My husband and I prayed about it and brought it before the Lord, and I did what the Lord told me to do. We had two little booklets, one about healing scriptures and one on scriptures to build up faith because faith is what I needed desperately for the time that was to come,

In April, I committed my mornings to the Lord so I could spend more time with Him and be in the Word.

Those mornings became very precious to me, and His presence increased in me. I loved it. It was worth every minute to spend that time with the Lord.

A Black Spot Was Growing

On the back of my left arm, there had always been a black spot. About six weeks from the time the Lord had given me that vision, I noticed the spot looked bigger than before. There was no doubt that it had started growing. We prayed for it and thought perhaps that was what I needed healing for. I trusted the Lord that He would take care of it. But that black spot became bigger, and in my heart, I knew it was cancer. No wonder the Lord had told me only to read scriptures about healing.

I kept on reading those healing scriptures and meditated on them so that the Word of God got in my heart. I started to believe that God was speaking to me through His Word. It says in Jeremiah 1:12, *"I am alert and actively watching over My Word to perform it."* I started to believe that He would perform His Word to me and bring healing to me when I put my faith in what God says in His Word. I also found a very interesting word in Deuteronomy 30:19–20, and I chose to live by it. It says: *"This day I call heaven and earth as witnesses against you that I have set before you life and death, blessings and curses. Therefore choose life, so that you and your children may live and that you may love the Lord your God, obey His voice and cling to Him. For He is your life and the length of your days."*

I firmly made a decision in my heart before the Lord Jesus and told Him, "Lord, from this day forward, I decide *to choose life,* to live according to Your Word, and to obey Your voice. In doing so, I am clinging unto You. I choose life instead of death. I choose blessings instead of curses." I did this with all my heart.

After I made that decision, the Holy Spirit guided me to Proverbs 4:20–22 which absolutely connects to that previous scripture. It says: *"My son, pay attention to what I say; listen closely to My words. Do not let them out of your sight, keep them within your heart; for they are life to those who find them and health to a man's whole body."* So, I thought, if God told me this, then through His written Word, healing and health will take place in my body. "My God," I said, "this is Your written Word. I believe it, and I will go for it!"

Healing and health are God's blessings to embrace!

Magnify Me, Not That Spot!

I also meditated on 1 Peter 2:24: *"He himself bore our sins in His body on the tree, so that we might die to sin and live for righteousness. By His wounds, you have been healed."* However, it wasn't always easy to trust the Lord; I had to go through a learning process. When I looked at that black spot, I saw that it was growing and not shriveling up like I thought it would. The Lord was so gracious in helping me through that process. Listen to what the Lord said to me one morning: "Don't magnify that spot, but magnify Me.

Don't look at it in fear but in the triumph of what I have already done for you on the whipping post and on the cross".

I had to think for a bit about what the Lord said to me, and after some time, I said, "Yes, Lord, yes. You are absolutely right! I have to magnify You and triumph in what You have done for me. Through Your wounds, You have already provided my healing. I am so sorry, Lord. I repent for the times when I have been fearful and not trusting in You and for what You have already done for me. I repent, O Lord. Please help me to go on in trust and in victory."

There are many healing scriptures, such as Matthew 8:16–17, Isaiah 53:4–5, Psalm 91, Galatians 3:13, Acts 10:38, and Isaiah 41:10. They are all promises from our Lord. They are life-giving. They bring healing and health to our mortal bodies, peace to our minds, and security for our hearts. I opened my heart to those scriptures until they became alive and real to me. John 3:16 says: *For God so loved the world that He gave His one and only Son, that whoever believes in him shall not perish but have eternal life.* It was through meditating on the love of the Father and on what He did for me in giving His Son to be crucified. And meditating on Jesus, who had to die a horrible death on the cross in order to give His precious blood to save and heal me. This demonstrated His incredible love for me. It touched me deeply, and I cried uncontrollably. At that moment I knew I could totally trust God and my Lord Jesus for my healing because they both love me that much!

The Blood of Jesus

In the meantime, the growth started to look awful and it was bleeding at times, so I had to cover it up with a bandage. I decided not to let my faith in God's Word and His love for me waver because His promises are yes and amen! One of those mornings, I took the bandage off and went in the shower. Suddenly, I saw blood from my arm dripping beside my feet. The moment I saw that blood, the Spirit in me rose up, and I shouted praise and thanked Jesus with my whole heart for His blood that had dropped on the ground while He was on the whipping post where those soldiers were ripping His back open for my healing. My Jesus suffered so much for me, and I was very thankful for his blood.

After the shower, I covered the spot up again, took my Bible, and started to read the chapters which describe the sufferings of Jesus. And again I was so thankful for all that Jesus willingly went through, shedding His blood for my salvation and healing. It installed in me a deep love for Jesus.

This Has to Be Taken off Quickly

I kept on believing and trusting the Lord at His Word, and my husband was in agreement with me. But by the end of July, he suggested that if that growth was not gone by the following week, we'd better go to the doctor to see what he thought about it. It was the first of August when we went to our family doctor, and from his face, we could see that it wasn't good at all. He said, "This has to be taken off quickly."

He made an appointment with a plastic surgeon to do a biopsy and remove the growth as soon as possible. He made it clear to the surgeon that this was very urgent.

I saw the surgeon a week later. He said, "This is very serious, and I will take this off quickly. I can't say what it is now because it could be one of two things, but first I have to do a biopsy before I can tell what it is. I do have to warn you ahead of time. It doesn't look good."

On August 16, the surgeon removed it and when he was done he said to me, "I have never seen such a big growth. I had to cut deep to remove it."

Four long weeks later, I went to his office for the results. He told me, "I don't have a good report for you." I can still see him standing against the counter in his office. "It is very serious; it is stage 4 melanoma. This kind of cancer is very aggressive. You never know where it will show up next. It can go through your whole body including your brain." When he said those words, faith rose up inside of me, and immediately these words came out of my mouth: "No it will not! The Lord is taking care of me. I trust my Lord."

The doctor looked at me kind of strange and said, "I will have to take action and will make an appointment with a cancer surgeon in the Juravinski Hospital in Hamilton. You will need to go through a scan and an MRI to find out what is going on in your body to see what to do next. They will call you and make an appointment with you. It will probably take three to four weeks." I, of course, agreed with that decision.

We Nullified the Report of the Doctor

At home, we prayed and did not accept that report from the doctor in our hearts. My husband took that report and slapped it on the table and nullified that melanoma stage 4, calling it void and speaking the report of what God says in His Word over my body. "God sent His Word and healed Ineke and delivered her from destruction. By His wounds she has been healed and made whole." (Ps. 107:20, Isa. 53:5) Also, we told the spirit of cancer to be removed from my body in Jesus' name!

I must say, I was in shock. I knew this growth wasn't good, but I didn't expect to hear such a bad report. At night, I couldn't sleep. I went to the Lord in prayer, and in my imagination, I went to the courtroom in heaven, to the throne of grace, and pleaded my case before the Judge of heaven and earth. I thanked Jesus that He was my advocate, that He gave His blood for my sins, and that by His stripes I had been healed from this cancer. I envisioned Jesus as my advocate, pleading my case before God, the Judge of heaven and earth. The Judge responded by saying, "Yes, Jesus, you are right. You have paid the price for Ineke, and she is cleansed, free from sin, and also healed as My Word says."

After this, I thanked the Lord and received peace in my heart over the whole situation, and I could sleep again. My husband didn't know about my endeavor with the Lord that night because I hadn't told him yet, but when Henk was praying that morning for me, the Lord showed him the inside of my arm. First he saw it with spots everywhere, and immediately after that the Lord showed him my arm again. This time it was totally clean—no spots at all. Hallelujah! Thank you, Jesus, for your encouragement and confirmation from what God said last night!

The Word Was and Is My Greatest Security

Still, every day, I kept on reading the healing Scriptures, and had to keep on trusting the Lord with my whole heart in order to stay in peace and lean on His understanding and not on my own understanding, thinking, or feeling. It was not always easy. I had to wait for weeks before the next step. I had to cling to the Word, and, yes, I chose the Word even above what Henk saw in the vision the Lord gave him: that my arm was clear. For me, the Word was and is my greatest security. We have flaws and can misinterpret things we see or hear, but *not* our Lord and *not* His Word. He is always right, and He is always the same. The Word is my rock. The Word is everlasting, and it never changes!!!

Like I said before, I was clinging to and choosing what the Scriptures said about my healing; otherwise fear and anxiety would have overtaken me. I had to learn, though, to stand strong against the enemy. I found out the only way I could be strong against his attacks was through the Word of God. I stood with the Word, as Jesus did when He was tempted by Satan. Jesus quoted Scripture and said to him, "It is written." Many times Satan came to me with doubt and fear, and I would tell him: *"I am not listening to your fear, unbelief, and doubt. I am only listening to the Word of my God, which says; It is written, that by the stripes of Jesus I am already healed, whether I see or feel it or not."* Also Philippians 4:6 says, *"It is written, don't be anxious about anything."*

Satan reminded me of my mom. She had cancer and had a double mastectomy. All six of my mom's sisters died from cancer and also one of her brothers. Also, my cousin had melanoma and died very quickly after he was diagnosed. I pondered on it for a bit. But then I said: "No chance, devil. I have a new inheritance; the old was broken off a long time ago when I became born again. I am now born of God. I am an heir of God and a joint-heir with Christ" (Rom. 8:17). Also, I said: "I am not under the curse anymore," and rebuked Satan with Galatians 3:13 that states: "Christ has redeemed me from the curse of the law. He had been made a curse for me."

Every day, I decided to trust the Lord through His Word. You know, we cannot see God but we can see and hold His Word in our hands and read about His perfect will, His desire, and His love for us.

The Lord encouraged me a lot through His Word in different places in the Bible. Sometimes it was as if He spoke directly to me. Once it was through Psalm 3:1-5: *"O Lord how many are my foes! How many rise up against me! Many are saying of me, God will not deliver him. But you, O Lord are a shield around me, my glory and the lifter of my head. To the Lord, I cry aloud and He answers me from His holy hill. I lie down and sleep, I wake again, because the Lord sustains me."*

Chapter 6:

Healed Forever!

Another time, I was reading my Bible and saw the word *forever*. First those letters were just normal, but then they became big in front of me—*FOREVER*—and this thought came to me: *I am healed forever, not healed yesterday and today sick again and then tomorrow healed again. No, I am healed forever*! God's Word is forever. God's love is forever. Jesus Christ is always the same yesterday, today, and forever.

This word *forever* made me strong against doubt and unbelief because I knew I had a death sentence over my head. Many times the Lord comforted me with His love through the book of Ruth, and that strengthened my faith also.

I love the book of Ruth. Ruth is an example to me because she surrendered her life totally over to the God of Naomi, the God of Israel, whom she did not know before. God honored that commitment and showed His love to her through Boaz. Boaz comforted her heart; he protected and cared for her. He fed her and also provided for both Naomi and her. Boaz showed the love of Jesus and became her kinsman-redeemer. Boaz is a foreshadow of Jesus as our

Kinsman Redeemer. I have read that story many times, and when I was reading it, several times His love overflowed my heart, and I started crying and weeping before the Lord. There is nothing more touching and beautiful than the love of Jesus. Our Kinsman Redeemer has spread the corner of His garment over us, His wings of protection, and He has offered His covenant to us. We are safe, protected, loved by Him, cared for, and forgiven. How I love Jesus, the Redeemer of my soul!

Juravinski Hospital

It took another four long weeks before the appointment with the doctor at the Juravinski Hospital. This doctor gave me the same report, but with an even stronger warning to prepare me for the worst. The doctor said, "This kind of cancer is the most aggressive cancer. It will go to your brain and through your whole body." Just as strongly as this warning came, before I realized it, I replied very strongly back to her with the words: "No, it will not. The Lord is taking care of me." The doctor looked at me strangely and said the same thing as the plastic surgeon said to me: "But I have to take action." She scheduled a scan and an MRI to determine how much the cancer had spread and what the next steps of action would be.

First of all, when we came home from that visit, we canceled the predictions of the doctor over my life and asked God for cleansing through the blood of Jesus. Then we cried out to the Lord, our strong tower, and pleaded for His grace over me. We spoke in tongues for a while and praised God for His love and care for us. During that time of praise, we both got refreshed, and Henk got a vision from Acts 28:3-6 about what happened to Paul in Malta. He saw that Paul got a pile of sticks and laid them on the fire, and because of the heat, a viper had crawled out of it and fastened itself on his hand. Henk saw that viper hanging on his hand and then being shaken it off into the fire.

We looked up that scripture and found it in Acts 28. *But Paul shook the viper off into the fire he suffered no evil effects. The people expected him to swell up or suddenly fall over dead, but after waiting a long time and seeing nothing unusual happen to him...* Suddenly I said to Henk, "That will happen to me too. The doctors will look and look but will find nothing that will harm me. I will not suffer any evil effect from this cancer nor die just like Paul!"

Hallelujah, I believe My Lord. He is the same God as in the life of Paul.

Waiting Again

Again, I had to wait before I was able to go for the scan and MRI. I thank God from the bottom of my heart that He was with me all the time. I continued to declare the Word of the Lord over my body because His Word is life and health. His Word is active, working out, as it says, if we just believe and lay hold of it. The enemy was active, too. His voice was loud, but the voice of my Lord was louder still. Hallelujah! Listen to this amazing word the Lord gave me from 2 Corinthians 2:14. In the Amplified version, it says: *"But thanks be to God who in Christ always leads us into triumph as trophies of Christ's victory."* It took me a while before I understood the depth of this incredible scripture because it is so amazing, so rich, so beautiful.

As a result of the suffering of Jesus on the whipping post and on the cross, Jesus won the victory over the devil and hell itself. And because of this, it clearly says that we are trophies. This is why Jesus could lead me in triumph as *his trophy*. At first, I could hardly receive this truth. Me, a trophy of Christ's victory? But when I received this word of Scripture, this truth in my heart, as a gift of grace from God for me, something happened in my heart. I became so happy and blurted out, *"I am a trophy of the Lord. I'm the fruit of His suffering. I am a trophy of the Lord. Hallelujah, glory to God!"*

This is the grace of God; we can't do anything to earn His grace. The only way to receive it is to accept what God has given us as a gift. He has chosen us to be His children and to be trophies of Christ's victory.

However, the one thing the Lord revealed to me is that we have to yield ourselves in total trust to what the Lord is doing in our lives. Yielding and trusting the Lord is a process; it takes time because most of us are wounded in our trust. But believe me, He will carry us through in His love, for it is the Lord's desire to restore and heal us in every way for His glory.

Remain in Me and I Will Remain in You

Yes, sometimes we go through the shadow of death, but when we realize were Jesus went through, all the suffering of constant rejection from his own people, the anguish of His soul in Gethsemane, the mocking of the soldiers, and the horrible death on the cross, than we can be triumphant with Him. He did it all out of love for us, to save us and heal us and make us His very own.

Nothing can stop us when we realize that our life, yes, the very breath in our mouth, comes from Jesus. Our heart then beats with the rhythm of the life of God Himself, our bones are strengthened daily, and every ligament that holds everything together in our bodies is carried through the cross. If we know that we live and move and have our being only in Jesus, then the only thing we want to do is thank Jesus in response and love Him back by pleasing Him and in obeying what His Word tells us to do.

Through pleasing and obeying the Word, I discovered the fellowship with Jesus is very sweet and His Word becomes a reality. John 15:1–17 says: "Remain in Me and I will remain in you. No branch can bear fruit by itself, but it must remain in the vine. Neither can you bear fruit unless you remain in Me." This is simple, but remaining in Him is not always easy because, over the course of time, the Father is pruning us. In this we have to be steadfast and endure in faith to stay in the vine, abiding in Jesus and not to go over into our flesh. When we remain in Jesus and when we remain in His Word and His love by doing His commands, we can ask whatever we wish and it will be given to us. "*This is to my Father's glory, that you bear much fruit, showing yourselves to be My disciples*" (John 15:8).

The same is to become His trophy. Dare to let Jesus do the work in you. He will guide, comfort, and strengthen you through your union with Him, in His Word and in prayer, praise, and thanksgiving. Also, through our obedience and reverence to God and to His Word, we will bless and honor Jesus for all the suffering He endured for us. Tell Jesus that you want to bear much fruit and that you want to be a trophy to the glory and honor of the Father.

Yes, this is what the Father wants us to be—*a trophy*. He will enable us to triumph over the enemy as *a trophy of Christ's victory*.

I Will Not Fail You

Finally, after more than three weeks of waiting, I could go in for the MRI. I wrote in big letters that scripture of being a *trophy of Christ's victory* on a piece of paper and put it in my pocket. And that is how I went into the machine for the MRI. Second Corinthians 2:14 was written on paper *but* also written in my heart. Three days later, I went for the full-body scan, again with that Scripture in my pocket and in my heart.

After we were home from the Hospital and when I was making supper, I pleaded with the Lord for strength because I felt so miserable from all the chemicals I drank in the last few days. At that moment, I heard the Lord's voice saying, *"I will not fail you."* "Oh, my Jesus," I blurted out, "You are so good, and I will shout this out to everyone who wants to hear how good you are!"

The very next morning (October 31) at 9:30 a.m., the receptionist from our family doctor's office called me. She told me, "The doctor wants to go over the report with you from the results of the scan and the MRI." That was the first time my heart sank. I thought, *when they call that soon, it must not be good.* For a bit, I was sitting kind of numb in my chair, but then I went with this phone call to my Lord who has always been my refuge, and I cast that heaviness on Him. Thank God, He gave me peace in this difficult moment.

But in the afternoon, I must say, I felt that anxiety and heaviness in my heart again when my husband and I got into the car to head to the doctor's office. Again, thanks be to God, that on the way to the office, the Holy Spirit came with His presence very strong upon me that my peace returned to me. Glory to my Lord!!! When it was our turn to see Dr. Manjos, he told us with a big smile on his face, "Don't worry; I have good news for you. Your MRI is totally clean, and so is your scan. They took photos of your whole body, and everything is clean, even your liver. There is not a cancer cell in your body or brain to be found."

The only thing I could say was, *"Thank you, Jesus, thank you, Jesus!"* over and over again. I was overwhelmed by God's goodness. The doctor was as happy as we were and went over the papers with us.

After two weeks, we received a call from the hospital to see the surgeon. When we came there, she was also happy

We Are *Trophies* Of *Christ's Victory*

for me and glad that she was able to give me good news. Many times she has to deliver bad news because stage 4 melanoma is deadly and inoperable, and she couldn't deny that it was a miracle. She said, "But we still have to do the procedure of cleaning up any trace cells that are invisible by a scan. It requires surgery. I have to cut two cm around where the growth was, and also remove two lymph nodes." She also said, "There could be tiny cells left that are only visible through a microscope." She wanted to make sure there were no cancer cells left.

I agreed to it, only because I know the tactics of the enemy. I know that over time, if I were to feel something at or around the place where that cancer was, the devil would come with his deceiving words and say, "There are still some cancer cells left; you should have had that procedure of cleaning up. You know that those lymph nodes are known for carrying cancer cells. Now you are in big trouble again." I knew that would happen, so that's why I agreed to that surgery.

As we drove home, my husband said, "They can't believe there is no trace of cancer. It's like the people I saw in that vision about Paul. They carefully watched Paul and expected him to die."

Again, There Were No Cancer Cells to Be Found

When I went for that surgery a few weeks later, I first had to go through a scan because they did not want to see any surprises while operating. After the operation, the surgeon went to my husband and told him that everything went well. The lymph nodes were all clean and also the spot where that cancer growth was, but she said, "I have to double-check with the microscope." Again, they kept on watching me.

After three weeks, the result of the operation was only good news. Glory to God! No cancer cells were found, not in the lymph nodes and not even in the area where the melanoma growth had been. But I must say—and I don't blame them at all—that in the hospital, it is difficult for the doctors to believe in miracles, and they actually expected the cancer would come back.

They recommended I should have chemotherapy treatments, which would take a whole year in order for me to have a better chance for the cancer not to come back, but they couldn't guarantee it. "No thank you," I said, "I didn't have any treatment before, and I won't take any treatment at this time either. Sorry, but no doctor has healed me nor can any treatment heal me either. It is the Lord who has healed me of this cancer, but I am thankful for what you have done for me." I sincerely thanked her for it.

The doctor said, "Well, we can't make you take treatments, but we would like you to come back for a check-up every six months. And, also, we want you to see a local doctor every six months to check your skin. In that way you are covered every three months."

"No thank you" I said again, "I am not coming back for that either because I am not expecting this cancer to come back. I'm not going to live in fear every three months." I had to sign for this decision and then we went home.

The Lord and His Wonderful Word Are My Guarantees

All the glory goes to the Lord who bore my sickness. This cancer was in His body on the whipping post, and by those wounds, I am healed from this awful cancer.

While I was writing this story (now six years later), the Lord reminded me of the time I saw the word *FOREVER* in my Bible. First, they were just normal letters, but then they became big while I was reading it. At the time that I went through this whole process, it really helped me stand strong against doubt and unbelief the devil was throwing at me. Now at this time, that word *forever* is sustaining me by letting me stand strong against the enemy's lies. Once in a while, he tries to tell me that this cancer will come back one of these days. But then, right away, I shout to him, "No way devil; it will never come back!"

Now, six years later, I still hold onto that word *FOREVER*. Everywhere around me, I see people with cancer that has returned, and I feel so sad for them. But I am so thankful that the Lord reminded me of that word, and I even heard at that moment His still, small voice saying, "You are healed and know this: it will not come back." Hallelujah! The Lord and His Word are my guarantee.

I am so glad that I spent so much time every morning with the Lord and His precious Word because now I understand how serious I need to take the Word. God speaks to me through His Word, and I understand that His Word has a great purpose. It lifts me up and encourages me; it blesses, instructs, and corrects me. It gives me peace and security. This is not only for me but for all of you who take the Word seriously.

If I had not spent all that time with the Lord, meditating and holding on His Word, believing and trusting it with my whole heart, I would have been in so much fear and anxiety. It would have overwhelmed me because of all the weeks I had to wait before I finally could go through the scan and MRI and then again waiting for the results. With the Lord, I triumphed over the enemy as a *trophy of Christ's victory*. Amen. All the glory goes to Jesus, my Healer and my Lord.

Author's Note and Prayer

I hope you are encouraged through my writing because my heart is going out to you who are battling with cancer. I also hope that you are encouraged to trust the Lord and get to know Him better through His Word because the Word of God is His heart—the Word is His desire for you. Open your heart to this truth, and let go and resist your fears about cancer because Jesus really cares for your well-being in His unending love for you. Have faith in Jesus; have faith in His Word. He is at your side. Victory always comes through your Lord Jesus who loves and cares for you.

We Are *Trophies* Of *Christ's Victory*

Father, I humbly come before You, and in Jesus' name I pray for your precious people who are looking to You for the healing of cancer in their bodies. Father, I pray that You guard their hearts and minds with peace in such a way that they are able to turn their eyes upon Jesus and receive the healing He brought forth through His suffering.

Lord, show yourself strong in the lives of your children and also in those who don't know You yet as Lord. Show to them Lord, that You are the One who rules, and not any kind of cancer.

And in Jesus' mighty name, I take authority over the spirit of cancer and command it to leave your body right now. Lord I pray, release your healing power for restoration in every cell that was destroyed through cancer. My Lord, I also pray for their strength to return in order to function again. Beloved, be healed of this cancer in the mighty name of Jesus! Amen, so be it!

Part 3:

She Will Not Die But Live

Chapter 7

The Lord Is Good, Gracious, and Faithful

I love telling you how good and gracious the Lord is, how much He loves us, and how faithful He is to His children. If we want to know how God thinks and how He does things, we just have to get to know His Word. When we get to know His Word, we become one with the Lord, and we start to think like Him in connection with His Word. His love and His abundant life flows through His Word into our hearts through reading and meditating on it together with the Spirit who lives in us.

God Saved My Life for a Second Time

I want to honor Jesus by telling you how He saved my life for a second time. Two nights in a row, I fainted. This was in the middle of March 2016. In the night, at two o'clock, I was not feeling well and went to the bathroom. There I fainted for the first time. My husband woke up from the bang and found me lying on the floor. He had to help me back to bed because I was too dizzy to walk by myself.

He prayed for me and, thank God, after his prayer, I could sleep again. The next day I was still not feeling well but trusted the Lord for my healing. The next night when I woke up, my stomach was turning, and I thought if I ate some yogurt I would feel better again.

I went to the kitchen, but I was so dizzy I could hardly find the light switch. When I realized I was going to faint again, I tried to sit down on the floor, but I was not fast enough and fell straight on my tailbone on the stone floor. In the process of losing my consciousness, I prayed, "Lord, cover me with Your blood and protect my head" because I could feel a strange feeling going up from my tailbone through my spine to my head, and it was a very scary feeling.

There in the kitchen, I was unconscious for some time, but I could hear Henk praying for me in tongues. He had been awakened from the bang on the floor. While Henk was praying for me, the Lord gave him a scripture from Isaiah 54:17: "No weapon that is formed against you will prosper." I could hear him speaking that word over me, and that was the answer to my prayer for the protection of my head, which gave me a big relief.

Henk had to carry me to bed because I was too weak to walk, and then beside our bed, I lost consciousness again. From that point on, I don't remember a thing. Henk could see and feel that I was dying in his arms, and he cried out to the Lord and spoke out the Scripture from Psalm 118:17: *"She will not die but live and declare the works of the Lord."* Through those words, my body became alive again. The words of God are powerful; they are life-giving and awesome. God's Word does what it says; it will not come back void. (See Isaiah 55:11.)

Henk helped me in bed and prayed earnestly for God's grace and peace to cover me so I could rest. I felt so dizzy, but the Lord gave me peace, and, amazingly I could sleep again. Henk told me, "Don't you dare to get out of bed by yourself again. If I am sleeping and you need to get up, you have to wake me up." Henk watched me like a hawk for months.

No Weapon That Is Formed Against Ineke Will Prevail

The day after this, Henk remembered what the Lord had said to him a few weeks earlier, that an attack of the enemy was coming our way. But of course, he had no idea that it would be so severe. The Lord also reminded me of a dream I had a couple of months before this had happened. In that dream, I woke up from a terrible storm blowing and beating against our house. I also heard rain clattering loudly against the window. Then in the dream, I heard myself praying, "Lord, please protect this house and also our lives; this is such a terrible, wild storm." I also heard Henk saying, "No weapon that is formed against Ineke will prevail."

Wow, I said to myself, *this is the same scripture Henk spoke over me when I was laying in the kitchen while I was unconscious.* To remember that was such an encouragement, as well as to know that the Lord was in all of this and that He knew that this would come our way. He even warned us before it would happen, in order that we could pray in advance. Knowing we were in God's care gave us peace. We kept thanking the Lord for His goodness in keeping us together and trusting Him no matter what. Yes, I was still dizzy, but I decided in my heart to trust God and said, "Jesus, I trust you with my life. You have proven Yourself twice already. First, melanoma stage 4 couldn't harm me, and now You saved my life again. Lord, you will make me healthy and strong for the plans you have for Henk and me. Have your way, Lord. I will follow you. Teach me your ways, in order to bear fruit in Your kingdom."

Fear Activated My Dizziness

The Lord taught me how to trust Him in the months that followed. I continued being dizzy, and those first weeks I was in bed or on the couch. The nights were the hardest because the enemy started working on my mind with fear. Because of that fear, the dizziness was activated even more. During those nights I couldn't sleep because sometimes I felt everything turning—myself and my bed—I thought about all the bad things that could possibly happen. The enemy is good at telling us bad things and all kinds of lies. What would I have done without the Lord?

In the midst of those nights, the Lord came in with his life-giving Word. He would give me a scripture verse, and when I meditated on it and spoke it out, faith came in and peace came over my mind so that I could sleep. When I would wake up again, I would press into that Word even harder and give myself totally over to the Lord in order to be in peace and not in fear. During the day, the Lord told me that this was not a sickness but a spiritual battle. I had to learn to totally give myself up and yield to the Word of God in what He was saying to me. I had to learn to put all my trust in Jesus and not listen to my feelings or fear.

One morning after a terrible night, I said to the Holy Spirit, "What do you think about this?" And right away the Holy Spirit said very sternly, "*Trust in the Lord with all your heart, and lean not on your own understanding*" (Prov. 3:5). Oh my, that word struck me in my heart; how true that was. I was leaning more on my own understanding and the bad things I heard from people. The Lord was absolutely right, and deep from my heart, I repented and asked forgiveness that I was not fully trusting Him in all His wisdom.

Right at that time, I recalled a scripture passage I read a long time ago. I knew it was in Proverbs somewhere, but I had to look it up in the concordance. I found it in Proverbs 3:21–26

> *My son, preserve sound judgment and discernment, do not let them out of your sight; they will be life for you, an ornament to grace your neck. Then you will go on your way in safety, and your foot will not stumble; when you lay down, your sleep will be sweet. Have no fear of sudden disaster or of the ruin that overtakes the wicked, for the Lord will be*

your confidence and will keep your foot from being snared.

That meant I didn't have to fear bad things or sudden disaster that overtakes the wicked. I am God's child and righteous through my Lord Jesus Christ. I can lay down in peace and sleep. The next night, however, was not any easier. It was still a fight for me to cling to His Word and not listen to my feelings. But scripture came to my mind from 2 Corinthians 2:4: "But thanks be to God, who in Christ always leads us into triumph." This helped me a lot and gave me peace, knowing that when I fully put my trust in God victory will always come, not bad or evil things. Through it, I found my refuge in the Lord and felt sheltered by Him. He was my embrace on that difficult night.

One More Night of This Battle

When I was talking to the Lord the next morning, He said, "One more night of this battle." I almost dreaded going to bed, but the Lord pulled me through that night also. In the morning when I was talking with the Lord, He said to me, "I am the mighty Conqueror. I am your conqueror, and in Me, you also are a conqueror! I will always lead you in triumph because I conquered death and hell. I triumphed over Satan and all his hosts. You have My power and authority in you; therefore use it!" The Lord is so wonderful; He will always encourage us.

The Lord Is Good, Gracious, And Faithful

There are a few other scriptures the Lord gave me at that time. When we take note of the Scripture and meditate on them one by one, they start to make so much sense. We need to act personally on the Word the Lord gives us to stand on, and through it we will overcome.

First Peter 5:8–9 says, *Be self-controlled and alert. Your enemy, the devil goes around like a roaring lion looking for someone to devour. Resist him standing firm in the faith.*

In John 16:33 Jesus says, *"In Me, you have peace. In this world, you will have trouble, tribulations, and trials, but take heart I have overcome the world."*

Revelation 3:5 tells us, *He who overcomes will, like them, be dressed in white.* This means that we have to overcome. And we will overcome if we hold onto the Word of life and yield to the One who has already overcome.

Finally, in Luke 10:19, the Lord says, *"I have given you authority to trample on snakes and scorpions and to overcome all the power of the enemy, and nothing will harm you."* His power, His authority, and His strength will prevail in every situation when we yield ourselves to Him who has given us that authority. When we yield to the Lord, we will become one with Him—one with the great Conqueror.

During that time, the Lord also showed me a road sign, a yield sign. I saw two roads, and then one road yielded to the other, and I saw the two roads becoming one. The Lord said, "That is how you become one with Me, in giving up your ways of doing things into My way of doing things. Give up your own thinking to bring it into conformity to My Word." In other words, we receive the mind of Christ and become one with Him when we yield ourselves to Him and His Word.

If we start to understand with our heart that the Word is given to us by God Himself and start to understand how to live according to His Word, it will help us to know how to react and trust the Lord in difficult situations. And on top of that, it will also give us peace and security. When we act on the Word, our lives will be built on the rock, and we will not be moved or blown over by the storms of life. Jesus tells us in Matthew 7:24–25: *"Therefore everyone who hears these words of Mine, and puts them into practice is like a wise man who built his house on a rock. The rain came down, the streams rose and the winds blew and beat against that house, yet it did not fall. Because it had its foundation on the rock."* That passage helped me so much. But at times it was still very hard, and I had to cling to those scriptures with my whole being.

A couple of times, I had to fight to hold onto those words and had to pray in tongues not to faint again. I almost didn't dare to get out of bed those nights. But thank God for a praying husband, and I am proud of him for the way he helped me in those nights and stood with me in prayer and steadfast faith. The roaring lion did not prevail. Glory to God; He was on my side and pulled me through.

It was training time for me. I learned again how important and powerful the Word is. As I said before, when we accept the Word as God's words and not words of men, then it does what it says (see 1 Thess. 2:13). God's Word is as powerful as God Himself. When I used the Word and meditated on it and spoke it out, it became my rock to stand on. Jesus said to his disciples in John 6:63, *"The words I have spoken to you are spirit and they are life."* In Proverbs 4:22 it says, *"For My Words are life to those who find them, and health to a man's whole body."*

When I got a hold of those words in my heart, it became easier to trust what the Word says. Yes, it will do what it says, no matter how I feel, or how fearful I was at times. I literally chose to trust God's Word because I knew that if I didn't, I would end up in the hospital and go through all kinds of tests. I wanted to trust my God my Healer.

(Hear me: this was my decision. I will say to nobody that it is not good to go to a doctor or to the hospital in one way or another.)

Wounds of Fear

One time, when Henk was praying for me, the Lord said to him, "Through all this, I am healing Ineke from the wounds of fear from her childhood, and I am also setting her free from a stronghold of fear."

I lived in so much fear when I was growing up because I was molested by my father when I was four and again when I was twelve. That fear was a part of me.

Praise the Lord that He has healed me over the years from all those deep wounds, but I had no idea that you could also have wounds from fear. But when I thought about it, it made a lot of sense. Also, I had a stronghold of fear that was built up through the years; no wonder that fear was always a part of my life. Praise the Lord, it isn't anymore! The Lord has delivered me from that stronghold during the process of my healing.

Still, I felt dizzy. This had been going on for almost three months at this point. Some days were better, and I felt like I could do something and was enjoying doing it, but then I did too much, and that left me dizzy for the next day unable to do anything. In all of this time, I knew this was an inner healing process and testing of my faith and *not* that the Lord was mad at me in any way. That was the reason I think that I could handle it and not doubt the Lord for loving me.

One morning I was reading Isaiah 12:2–3, and that scripture gave me so much joy. It says: *"Surely God is my salvation, I will trust and not be afraid. For the Lord God is my strength and song. Yes, he has become my salvation. Therefore with joy, you will draw water from the wells of salvation."* Wow, it says with joy you will draw water from the *wells* of salvation. When I was reading this, I understood that salvation has different wells, not only the well of forgiveness, but also a well of healing and deliverance, a well of joy and peace, and a well of prospering our souls.

There are so many aspects of our salvation. Those are wells, and they are deep and glorious. I was laughing and drinking from that refreshing water of the Word. It strengthened me, and I felt much better. I also thought of another scripture, Hebrews 5:9 (Amp) which says, *He became the Author and the Source of eternal salvation to all those who give heed and obey Him.* I looked up the meaning of the word *source*, and it says it is a spring from which a stream flows. Wow, how true that is; Jesus is the beginning and the spring of living water, our source of Life! And that spring is constantly flowing in all its power. It gives us eternal life, healing, deliverance, joy, peace, refreshment, and all the good things that come from God. The Lord offers us salvation in all its fullness, and it is up to us to receive it and drink from those wells. Hallelujah, I was drinking from that refreshing well that morning and was satisfied.

I Desperately Wanted to Work in Our Garden

By now it was the middle of June. I wanted to go outside and work in our backyard with Henk, which I love to do. But I still felt dizzy most of the time and could not do what I had always done, such as enjoying time together in our garden. I went to the doctor for the first time to find out why I was so dizzy. At that time I didn't mention that I had passed out three times and almost died but a year later, I did tell the doctor the whole story. He listened carefully and said to me twice, "This is the power of prayer."

The doctor took my blood pressure, which had always been perfect, but it wasn't then. It was much too high, and he gave me medication and told me to come back to his office a week later. After a week, I felt a bit better, but my blood pressure was still too high. In spite of it, I prayed and praised the Lord that it would come down to 120/80 and stay that way. I had to check it every day, and soon it began to come down to the right level. Then I started skipping doses for a few days, but my blood pressure would go up again. After taking the capsules again for a couple of days, my blood pressure was too low. I constantly had to check it. I was dizzy when it was too high, and I was dizzy when it was too low.

I cried out to the Lord with my whole heart and said, " You are my Lord, and I want to be led by You and not be controlled by blood pressure checks all the time." Then, as always, I went to my Bible because that is my stronghold and my security. In Romans 6:4 it says, "*Just as Christ was raised from the dead, through the glory of the Father, we too may live in newness of life.*" Also in 1 Corinthians 15:57, it tells us the Lord will always lead us into victory through our Lord Jesus who won the greatest victory ever on the cross and in hell over Satan and his demons. So I knew I would overcome, too. Then the Holy Spirit made clear to me *to be patient.*

By that, I understood that even in trouble, I need to have a victorious attitude. I said, "Okay, Lord, I decide to be that way because the Holy One is in me, and I can have a victorious attitude in this trouble. The roaring lion will not prevail." I started to laugh and quoted Psalm 91:13: "*You (*that means me*) will tread upon the lion and the cobra, and trample the great lion and the serpent.*" And I shouted, "You devil, you will not prevail in my life. I will conquer you by the blood of the Lamb and the word of my testimony, which is the Word of God."

I did as Jesus did when He rebuked the devil with the words "It is written" and quoted Scripture to him, and the

The Lord Is Good, Gracious, And Faithful

devil left Him. O yes, *I trampled on my enemy but bowed down deep for my Lord and Savior because Jesus is the one who gives me the victory through His precious Word and His incredible love.*

Through the years, the Word of God has become ever precious to me. I knew that I had to act on His Word to get me out of sickness and trouble.

It Was Always the Word That Gave Me Victory

I learned this because of everything I had gone through. Yes, it has always been the Word that has brought me through. It was always the Word that gave me victory and security. Even when I was diagnosed with melanoma stage 4 cancer in 2012, it was the Word that gave me faith and strength to hold on to God's promises, and it taught me that healing was paid for by Jesus' precious blood. I learned to hold onto the Lord and persevere with His Word. As my sins were wiped away, cleansed through the blood of Jesus, so the cancer was wiped out of my body by His blood and the wounds Jesus suffered for me. Thank you, Jesus, it's all because of You! Through my experiences, I learned to live by and with the Word, no matter what I felt, what people said, or what the doctor said.

When we make a decision and are determined to let the Lord accomplish things in our lives, it gives us so much fulfillment, joy, and security. Also, with our decision and determination, we honor the Lord and make Him number one in our lives. I must say this is not the easiest path. It takes a lot of patience and endurance, and sometimes we will ask, "Lord, is this really the way to go? Am I hearing you right?"

First Peter 5:10-11 was a great encouragement to me. It says: *"And the God of all grace, who called you to his eternal glory in Christ, after you have suffered a little while, will Himself restore you and make you strong, firm and steadfast. To Him be the power forever and ever amen."* Hallelujah, Jesus is working in my soul to be like Him and to be strong and immovable against the enemy, to be full of love and compassion toward my brothers and sisters and those who still need to come into His glorious light. I started to believe in my heart that victory always comes when I trust the Lord and put my faith in God's Word and not in the trouble I'm in.

I believed Jesus would always come to my aid during those times when I felt my heart pounding in my chest, as though I was about to have a heart attack, or when I was dizzy and felt the whole room turning. He gave me strength and peace and whatever I needed in those nights. I was always so thankful for His care and love for me. Yes, He is always good. He is not punishing us but building us up in our character, teaching us to have our trust and faith in Him all the time. Through trouble, we begin to know God's character, His patience, and His love for us.

Once, when I was reading, I landed on *"Stop doubting and believe"* in John 20:27. The Lord spoke those words directly to my heart as a rebuke, and the only thing I could do after this rebuke was repent of my doubt and unbelief. I am so glad that there is always forgiveness with Jesus

The Lord Is Good, Gracious, And Faithful

and that His love compels us to go on. Hallelujah! After I repented, I read Hebrews 4:2, and amazingly, this connected perfectly with what the Lord had just spoken to me. Listen to what it says: *"But the message the Israelites heard did not benefit them, because it was not mixed with faith."*

The Amplified Bible in this particular verse explains *faith* this way: *"The leaning of the entire personality on God in absolute trust and confidence in His power, wisdom, and goodness."* When I read that I thought, *That's exactly what it is,* and said, "My Lord, I still have a lot to learn, but I am thankful that You are so patient with me and are working on me to accomplish Your purpose for my life." The Bible always encourages us. As it says in 2 Corinthians 4:17–18, *"For the light and momentary troubles are achieving for us an eternal glory that far outweighs them all. So we fix our eyes, not on what is seen but what is unseen. For what is seen is temporary, but what is unseen is eternal."* This means God sees our trouble, our sickness, our persecution, or whatever our trial is *as light and just for a moment*, and glory to God, it will bring forth an eternal weight of glory. What a great and wonderful God we serve.

Also, Hebrews 10:35-36 is very encouraging: *"So do not throw away your confidence, it will be richly rewarded. You need to persevere so that when you have done the will of God, you will receive what he has promised."* Yes, all the promises of God are yes and amen, but we have to lay hold of them and be patient to receive what is promised.

Chapter 8

We Override A Problem With The Word Of God

In our thinking, we need to override the problem or pain we have through speaking and acting on what God says in His Word. Through our consistency, we overcome defeat, sickness, disease, pain, fear, and any other battle we might have to fight. In Revelation, John writes to each of the seven churches, *"Hear what the spirit says,"* and it also says, *"he who overcomes."* So it is very important that we listen to the Spirit, and in obeying, we will be overcomers.

As overcomers, no matter what the devil throws at us, he is defeated and, yes, stripped of his armor. We are conquerors because of the blood of Jesus. *"And they overcame him by the blood of the Lamb and by the word of their testimony"* (Rev. 12:11). The Lord gave me insight on what *"their testimony"* means, and this is what I understood: we are overcomers by what Jesus has done for us already. It is actually the testimony of Jesus, what He did in shedding His blood for us in order for all of us to be conquerors through Him.

I also understood that the blood of Jesus is still crying out ***victory*** in and for our lives. This is so important and valuable to know that the blood of Jesus has a voice and is crying out *victory* on our behalf. Look at what it says in Genesis 4:10, where we clearly can see that blood has a "voice." Listen to what the Lord was saying to Cain: *"Your brother's blood cries out to Me from the ground."* When I read that, something opened up in me, and the Lord revealed this to me: the blood of Abel was crying out *vengeance*, but the blood of Jesus was and still is crying out *victory*. His blood is crying out *victory* for us, and when we know that victory is ours, it gives us strength and security against the attacks of the enemy.

There is a song we used to sing in Holland, and I started singing that song aloud with my whole heart. It goes like this: "O how wonderful is Jesus' blood, O how wonderful is Jesus' blood. The power of the devil is broken through His might, O how wonderful is Jesus' blood." When I was singing that anointed song, I felt God's power was flowing inside of me, and I felt that I could easily conquer the enemy with the blood of Jesus. Yes, there is mighty power in the blood of Jesus!

My Heart Exults and Triumphs in the Lord

Several times, the Holy Spirit gave me 1 Samuel 2:1–2 (AMP) to read. It's Hannah's prayer where she said, *"My heart exults and triumphs in the Lord. My horn is lifted up in the Lord. My mouth is no longer silent, for it is open wide over my enemies because I rejoice in Your salvation. There is none holy like the Lord, there is none besides You. There is no rock like our God."* I absolutely loved it, and I shouted out those two verses in the joy of the Lord. It gave strength and victory inside of me. What a prayer for each of us when we face hard times, when we are down or depressed. It gives us such a boost when we open our hearts and mouths and shout out praises to our Lord and declare who Jesus is. By doing this, we also shut the mouth of our enemy. Hallelujah, glory to God!!!

The Narrow Road

At this point, you may be thinking, *Now she will be totally fine again*, but no, battles kept coming. Most of the time, I was still dizzy. One morning I said to the Lord, "I give myself totally up to You. I can't go on like this anymore. I am done, and my life is Yours. Your Word says, 'I died and my life is now hidden with Christ in God' (see Colossians 3:3.) That's how I feel, Lord; that's where I'm at. It is not I but You Lord. Strengthen me to go on." Then I remembered a vision the Lord gave me a couple of years after I came to Him. I saw myself vomiting flesh; I literally saw flesh coming out of my mouth. At that time, the Lord gave me His Scripture that says flesh and blood cannot become partakers of eternal salvation and inherit the kingdom of God (see 1 Cor. 15:50). Now I understand the total giving up of ourselves, and I also know that it is not easy.

We Are Trophies Of Christ's Victory

As Jesus said in Mark 10:15, *"I tell you the truth, anyone who will not receive the kingdom of God, like a little child, will never enter it."* Also, in Mark 10:24-27, we see where Jesus said to His disciples, "Children, how hard is it to enter the kingdom of God! Matthew 7:13–14 says, *"Enter through the narrow gate for wide is the gate and broad is the road that leads to destruction, and many enter through it. But small is the gate and narrow the road that leads to life, and only a few find it."* I want to belong to those few. How about you?

I came to understand that our Christian walk is not an easy road. We have to give up our matured will and become like children again to trust, love, and obey our heavenly Father. We have to yield ourselves to God and come into conformity to the likeness of Jesus, His Son (see Rom. 8:29). I know this goes deep, but I am just telling you what Jesus has taught me in my suffering and pain through the years. When we really want to go all the way with Jesus, He makes it possible for us to walk that narrow road and enter into the gate of his kingdom. I tell you, it is worth every step!

Eternity is forever. There are two options: forever in the hot flames of hell or forever in the joy of the Lord and in God's glorious presence in heaven. The choice is ours. Jesus did his part in shedding His blood, hereby opening the way to God our Father because His desire is that all men be saved (see 1 Timothy 2:4). Walking in His way is our part.

I Saw Feet Dragging in the Dirt

One morning, the Lord gave me a vision. I saw two feet dragging in the dirt. I knew in my spirit that they were the feet of Jesus. What I saw was Him carrying the cross and exhaustedly dragging his feet through the dirt of a dusty road. He could hardly put one foot in front of the other. Then I shouted out, "Oh, my Jesus, You know exactly what it is to be exhausted, so tired and weary that You can hardly go on." That is how I felt at that moment. I was so exhausted and tired, but my Lord carried that all for me and for you as well.

My heart went out to the Lord, and I said, "You are so amazing. How could You go through all the suffering?" And suddenly I knew that Jesus also had to totally depend on His Father for His strength in every moment. When Jesus was walking this earth, He was human like us, only without sin. No wonder it says in the Psalms so many times that God is our strength. He is our stronghold. He is the strength of our life. This is so good for all of us to realize and to get into our spirits *that He is our strength, so we don't depend on ourselves but on the Lord.* He knows exactly what we are going through. He knows when we are tired, weary, exhausted, and when we are oppressed or even depressed. Jesus bore everything for us, so we can cry out to Him for all that we need. I found out the Lord strengthens us through singing praises to Him and through reading the Scriptures.

Some of those *strengthening scriptures,* as I call them, are:

Psalm 68:35: *"You are awesome oh God in your sanctuary, the God of Israel gives power and strength to his people."*

Psalm 73:26: *"My flesh and my heart may fail, but God is the rock, and firm strength of my heart and my portion forever."*

Psalm 18:1: *"I love you, oh Lord my strength."*

Psalm 18:32: *"It is God who arms me with strength and makes my way perfect."*

Psalm 18:39: *"You armed me with strength for battle."*

Psalm 46:1 *"God is our refuge and strength, an ever present help in trouble.*

Psalm 59:17: *"Unto you, oh my strength, I will sing praises, for God is my defense, my fortress, and high tower."*

Isaiah 40:29-31 is also very good and well known: *"He gives strength to the weary and increases the power of the weak. Even youths grow tired and weary, and young men stumble and fall. But those who hope in the Lord will renew their strength. They will soar on wings like eagles; they will run and not grow weary, they will walk and not faint."*

You might say, I know all those scriptures, but it doesn't do anything for me. O yes, I know what you are saying, but I have learned to meditate on the Scriptures and open my heart to them in order for the Holy Spirit to make them alive in me and empower my soul and my body through them. Proverbs 4:4 says it clearly: *"Lay hold of My Words with all your heart; keep My commands and you will live."*

Yes, it takes time to meditate on the Word and let the presence of the Lord become real and alive in us. But it absolutely pays off to take time with the Lord every day. Sometimes when I read my Bible, suddenly the Holy Spirit comes over me with His wonderful presence, and I start to weep from deep within. At moments like that, I know the Lord is speaking to me through His Word something I need to discover or provide healing of my soul. Sometimes the Lord gives me a revelation of the Scripture I am reading, and then suddenly I understand what that passage is telling me. *Jesus is the Word, and He is talking to us through His Word.*

The Lord also reveals things to me in visions. This is so precious and means everything to me. The Lord means more to me than the whole world could offer. We get empowered through that union with the Lord and His Word. But also in prayer, we draw strength from Him, which His boundless might provides. That is exactly what it says in Ephesians 6:10 (AMP). I love to spend my mornings with the Lord and my Bible. My faith has grown so much through those times, and I have begun to really believe the Word. I believe those words in the Bible are the truth and are for me. *The Word is a lamp to our feet and a light for our path* (see Psalm

119:105). When we follow the light of the Word, it will expel all the darkness, sickness, and disease in us.

Every day I still declare some of those strengthening scriptures and also the healing scriptures. The Lord taught me that when I had cancer—actually before I knew anything about this melanoma on my arm—the Lord warned me to read healing scriptures. He said, "Read the healing scriptures, forget all the other ones; read only the healing scriptures." I did, and the result is that I am healed and alive today.

Also, I learned to ask the Lord for wisdom and revelation every day, like Paul as he was praying for the people in Ephesians 1:17: *"I keep asking that the God of our Lord Jesus Christ, the glorious Father, may give you the spirit of wisdom and revelation so that you may know Him better."* If Paul told the people to keep asking the Lord for wisdom and revelation, I thought I should do that as well. I am encouraging you to do the same because there is nothing more exciting than when the Lord gives us revelations and visions about His Word.

God Is My Almighty, Loving Father

Now I'd like to tell you about the wounds that I didn't realize were still in my soul. Thank God, He knew exactly the healing I needed from the fear of my childhood. When I was praying one morning, the Lord put on my heart to read from a book by Corrie ten Boom. She was telling of how her loving father helped her overcome the fear of leaving the protection and the warmth of her home on the first day of school. She cried and was afraid to leave, but her father, who knew her fears, took her by the hand and led her into the unknown world of school and teachers.

In my mind, I went back to my early school years. I too was fearful, shy, and full of insecurity. Corrie had a loving father who helped her through it, but I didn't have that. Then suddenly, a thought welled up in me, and I just blurted it out: "But you, O God, are my Father, my almighty, loving Father." At that moment, I realized my heavenly Father had taken my hand and carried me through all my fears, insecurity, and pain that I had lived in all those years. I could feel His love at that moment, and I started to cry. I was sobbing, and healing took place deep in my soul when I felt His loving care for me, knowing that God was my only refuge. His everlasting arms have always been carrying me through.

What a revelation that was when I discovered that my heavenly Father has always been with me to this very moment. I was so thankful to know and experience that deep and loving care, and at that moment peace filled my heart. I had peace instead of fear by knowing that He always had been watching over me, always had been caring for me, always loved me. And even still, my heavenly Father is watching over me, caring for and loving me, no matter what is happening in my life. He will carry me through until I am in my heavenly home, forever living in peace, security, love, and joy. What sweet comfort!

Chapter 9

Trust Me All The Way

Still, I didn't feel well at all. I continued to be dizzy, and I asked the Lord, "Do you want me to go to a doctor or naturopath?" Right away, the Lord said in my heart, *"Trust me all the way."* I said, "Okay, Lord, I will trust You all the way!"

Because I wanted to be sure that I heard from the Lord, I also asked my husband if he would ask the Lord if I should go to a doctor or naturopath. And this is what the Lord said to him: *"No, don't let her go!"* So that was clear enough, and I said again, "All right, Lord, I trust you all the way! I give myself and my body as a living sacrifice to You according to what Romans 12:1 says: *"Therefore, I urge you, brothers, in view of God's mercy, to offer our bodies as a living sacrifice, holy and pleasing to God, which is your spiritual worship. Do not conform any longer to the pattern of this world, but be transformed by the renewing of your mind. Then you will be able to test and approve what God's will is. His good, pleasing and perfect will."*

At church, they always asked how I was doing. I answered, "Well, I am not there yet, but Jesus is my head, and His head is good and perfect, and that is why I am good, too. Jesus is doing an eternal work in me, and eternity is very long in comparison with this little time on earth." A sister in the Lord said to me, "Ineke, I am not praying for you anymore because the Lord said to me, 'Don't pray for Ineke because I am doing holy work in her; just leave it up to Me.'" That was a wonderful encouragement and also a confirmation of what I had said many times—that the Lord is doing an eternal work in me.

One morning I was reading 1 Kings 8:56 that says, *"Not one word has failed of all His good promises, which He has promised."* When I was reading this, the Lord touched my heart, and I knew the Lord was speaking to me that He would never fail in one word of His promises to me. I absolutely love it when He touches me; His presence and His love are so real in those moments.

A couple of weeks later, the miracle of the fulfilling of the Lord's promise about "trusting Him all the way" happened like this. I said to the Lord that morning, "This is crazy; I keep having to check my blood pressure to see whether it is too high or too low. Whatever I take—a whole capsule, a half a capsule, or nothing— it is never right. Lord, I don't want to be controlled by my blood pressure. I want You to control me because You are my Lord, and I am under Your Lordship and *not* under the lordship of the devil and sickness anymore. I am Your child. I live in Your Kingdom, and I know very well that the Father has drawn me to Himself and delivered me out of the control and dominion of darkness. He has transferred me into Your Kingdom of light. I don't live in the darkness anymore, therefore, I take my blood pressure out and away from the control and dominion of darkness in Jesus' name. Now I place my blood pressure into Your light and under Your Lordship. From now on I am asking *You* to control my blood pressure."

And you know what? That is what happened from that moment on. Jesus took control of my blood pressure, and it became stable. Within a week my blood pressure was totally fine, and it still is. Praise be to Jesus, my Healer and Deliverer. He is so good and shows Himself strong and faithful when we live by His Word and pray according to His Word.

Interceding with Psalm 118:17

A week later in my devotion with the Lord, I was thanking Him that I was still alive and hadn't died, and that the Lord would be with us in all the plans He has for me and my husband before His return to take His bride with Him to heaven into the new Jerusalem. While I was worshipping the Lord, He reminded me of the fact that at the beginning of the year, I was interceding for somebody with Psalm 118:17. At that time, I was reading a book about a testimony of someone who was prompted by the Holy Spirit to pray while he was on his way to a board meeting of his church. He started to intercede and the words, "She will live and not die" came out of his mouth loudly.

While I was reading this, the Holy Spirit came over me so strongly and from deep within those words of Psalm 118:17 came out of my mouth as well, with power and authority. *"She shall not die, but live and declare the works of the Lord."* I repeated them over and over. *"She shall not die, but live and declare the works of the Lord,"* not knowing for who I was interceding, but I knew it was the Spirit of God directing me to do so. When I felt victory in my spirit and knew that my prayer was accomplished, I picked up the book again and underlined the story with the date of my interceding and put it away.

"Oh yes, Lord, I sure remember that I was interceding for someone, but I have no idea for whom I had been praying." At that moment I heard the Lord saying, "Ineke, you were interceding for yourself with those words from Psalm 118:17." I was shocked when the Lord said that. "Really Lord is that true? I have never heard that you can intercede for yourself!" Well, I thought, *How could you know months ahead what will happen in your life, and what you need prayer for?* "Please, Lord," I asked, "Can you confirm this to me because I will never tell anyone this if I'm not sure that this is true." While I was talking to the Lord, I took that book from the shelf and said, "But Lord, where can I find that story? I have no idea about which page I read it." (The book has over 300 pages.) Amazingly, when I opened the book, it opened exactly to the page where it was written in bold letters and underlined in bright pink the words **"SHE WILL LIVE AND NOT DIE."** The date was January 20, 2016.

Right away, before I could even think, the Lord touched me so deep that I started to cry, and in my heart I knew, yes, I had interceded for myself. I shouted out, "Lord, You are incredible! Thank you, Lord, you are incredible!" It was so overwhelming to me the only thing I could say was, "You are incredible," over and over again. Also, I thanked the Lord for confirming this so mightily in my heart. This was very precious to me!

In the afternoon, I was still overwhelmed about the things the Lord told me and revealed to me that morning. I went back to my prayer room, and while I was sitting in my chair praising the Lord, He said to read Psalm 41. I read it in the Amplified Bible. Listen to what it says: *"Blessed is he who considers the weak and the poor; the Lord will deliver him in the time of evil and trouble. The Lord will protect him and keep him alive; he shall be called blessed in the land and You will not deliver him to the will of his enemies. The Lord will sustain, refresh and strengthen him on his bed of languishing and will restore him from his bed of illness."*

Again I was touched. Those words were revealing my heart because my heart always goes out to the weak, to the hurting, and to the poor people. Psalm 41 also confirmed the reality of what had happened in the past six months. The Lord had delivered me from evil and trouble. He had protected me and kept me alive and did not let the enemy triumph over me. He had given me the strength to go through everything, and He had restored me totally. What a beautiful confirmation of my healing.

How Can We Tell All His Wonderful Deeds?

Psalm 106:1-2 (Amp.) says: *"Give thanks to the Lord for he is good. His love endures forever. Who can put into words and tell the mighty deeds of the Lord? Or who can show forth all the praise that is due to Him?"* How true this scripture is for me. How can I put into words and tell the wonderful and mighty deeds the Lord did in me during this time? It is incredible how He spared my life for the second time, and how He healed me from the wounds of fear from my childhood. All the dizziness is gone, I am not weak anymore, and I am strong. I am totally healed from high blood pressure, and most of all, the Lord taught me again to trust Him in such a deep way that it is hard to explain with words. I learned to believe Him and yield to the words He gave me in the middle of the night, and to put my faith in these words and not to lean on my own understanding.

Hallelujah, God's Word and my faith in His Word brought me through those difficult nights to overcome the enemy.

There Were Three Angels Who Showed up in Our Bedroom.

While I was writing this, the Lord reminded me of something I experienced years ago. I had seen three angels who showed up in our bedroom and stood at the end of our bed. They were very tall and clothed in white. The first angel said to me, *"Shalom, Ineke."* And the second one said, *"Shalom, Ineke."* And the third also said, *"Shalom, Ineke."* Oh yes, Lord, I remember that very well. How could I ever forget that beautiful experience! Then the Lord responded to me and said, "There were three major attacks on your life.

The first one was on your liver (in 1996, I was diagnosed with incurable liver disease, and right now the doctors can not believe that I'm still doing good and well after all these years), the second attack was cancer, and the third attack was when you were at the point of death in Henk's arms. *Those three angels have spoken Shalom over you one by one in order that the spirit of death could not master you, Ineke."*

This made me speechless for a while. I was overwhelmed by what the Lord had revealed to me. I was overwhelmed just to know that the Lord would send three angels to speak *"Shalom"* over me so that I would *"not die but live."* I was also overwhelmed to know His plans were to prosper me and not to harm me. That is how marvelous the Lord is, not only for me but also for you.

Most of the time, we have no idea what is going on in the spirit realm, but it is much bigger and more wonderful than we can imagine. That's why it is necessary to pray and ask the Lord if He will open our eyes and ears for the spirit realm and also for revelation to know and understand His ways and plans for us. This makes our Christian walk so much more meaningful and exciting. The Lord loves to reveal Himself through His Word and through visions. He loves to show His goodness so we get excited about Him and His Word.

Author's Note and Prayer

In this part, you can clearly see that the Word of God is alive and does not come back to us void but to accomplish what it says and prospers in the thing where God sends it. Yes, He will create the fruit of our lips. The Lord loves it when we are patient and trust Him with all our hearts. He is our strength and our Healer. He knows all about us from our birth onward and even before.

At this moment, there is a song in my heart and the words are this: "There is none like You, no one else can touch my heart like You do. I can search for all eternity long and find there is none like You."

> *Yes, Lord Jesus, this is so true; there is no one like You who can touch our hearts in the right time and in the right way with your love in order to hold on and persevere in the trial we are in. O, my Lord, that's why I come to You in prayer for my dear brothers and sisters who are looking to You for healing in whatever way or form. Touch their bodies with your healing power like no one else can do! Lord Jesus, touch them deeply in their hearts with courage to hold on in faith to You and your Word. And also I pray for your strength to persevere because You will never fail them.*
>
> *With You, Lord Jesus, there is always victory coming, and the sting of sickness is gone, swallowed up in the victory You won over death, sickness, and disease.*

Therefore, I plead the blood of Jesus over you and pray in Jesus' name for healing in your body through the stripes Jesus bore for for you. Be healed precious child of God in Jesus' name, amen.

Part 4:

Put Me First

Chapter 10

The Warfare We Are In Is Real

The beginning of the fourth part of this book may be shocking to you, but I'm just writing down what the Lord showed me in a vision four or five days before I felt a rash on my back. In that vision, I saw an enormous big rat standing on his two back legs, and with his other two legs he embraced me. I could feel the pain of his sharp nails from one of his claws scratching my back just under my shoulder blades toward my side and my breast. After thinking over this, I said to myself, *this is not from the Lord. A rat is unclean, so definitely, this is from the enemy, but why did I see this? Is the Lord warning me about an attack from the enemy?* My husband also thought that it was not from the Lord, so I rebuked it and went on.

But four or five days later, I felt a rash on my back and asked the Lord to cleanse it with his blood, not at all thinking about the vision of that rat. I rebuked the rash and told it to be gone, but after a couple of days, it was still there. I looked in the mirror to see what it was because it started to be painful. I didn't know what it was but saw that it was more than a rash, and after another couple of days, it became very painful. After a good look in the mirror again, I could clearly see that it was bad, and then suddenly I realized that this rash was exactly in the place where that rat had his leg on my back. It was under my shoulder blades toward my side and breast. There were spots even under my breast, and again I had no idea what that rash could be. The only thing I knew was that the pain became very intense, so much so that I couldn't even keep my bra on.

My husband and I prayed. We rebuked that awful spirit and trampled it under our feet with the Word of God. But I have to say, it didn't help, and I could not understand why the rash didn't go away.

And You Will Win

After a couple of days, I spoke out loud the words of Colossians 1:13 (AMP): *"The Father has delivered and drawn me to Himself out of the control and out of the dominion of darkness and has transferred me into the kingdom of the Son of His love."* I established those words in my heart as absolute truth. And after that, the Lord responded to me, *"Hold onto this Word in every hard and every difficult situation, and you will win."*

Then my mind went to Ephesians 6:10–14:

> Finally, *be strong in the Lord and His mighty power. Put on the full armor of God so that you can take your stand against the devil's schemes. For our struggle is not against flesh*

and blood, but against the rulers, against the authorities, against the powers of this dark world and against the forces of evil in the heavenly realm. Therefore put on the full armor of God so that when the day of evil comes you may be able to stand your ground, and after you have done everything, to stand. Stand firm then with the belt of truth buckled around your waist.

Another translation says, *"Having tightened the belt of truth around your waist."* For me this means that we have to make sure that we have the truth of the Word firmly settled in our hearts.

"But Lord," I said: "why do I have this, and why did I see that unclean rat?" Again the Lord responded and said, "I want you to know how real the spiritual realm is; *stand your ground.*" A couple of days went by, and one night the pain was quite intense. Because the pain was not only on my back but also under my breast, I started to be fearful. This fear entered my heart because I didn't know what this rash was all about.

I know the fear made it worse, and I couldn't handle it anymore, so early in the morning, we went to the emergency room.

The doctor told me that it was shingles and that shingles is very painful. He also said that if I would have come in right away when it started, he could have given me a shot and that would have stopped the process but not at this later stage.

He could do nothing for me. I had never heard of shingles, other than seeing a picture in a doctor's office. Now that I knew what it was, I could handle it better. Actually, believe it or not, I was glad they didn't give me medication because I really don't like to take medication, and now I could fully set my heart on the Lord for my healing. The Lord bore this pain already on His back, and by those wounds that Jesus suffered, I am healed. The wounds and pain on His back were far more painful than my pain, and that encouraged me. So I trusted Jesus for my healing.

A song came to my heart: "Turn your eyes upon Jesus. Look full in His wonderful face, and the things of this world (which includes sickness and pain) will grow strangely dim, in the light of His glory and grace." I had to look to Jesus, to the cross and His cleansing blood, and remember where Jesus went through to save me and heal me.

Tormented by Unclean Spirits

One morning, I was reading Acts 5:16: *"Crowds gathered also from the towns around Jerusalem, bringing their sick and those tormented by unclean spirits and all of them were healed."* O my, that phrase, *those tormented by unclean spirits*, struck me. I said to myself, that is exactly what that devil rat is and does; it is an unclean spirit and a tormenting spirit. That pain of shingles on my back is tormenting me, and that unclean spirit I saw in that vision is causing it!

The Amplified Bible says it is a foul spirit. I looked up in the dictionary what the meaning of the word *foul* is, and

The Warfare We Are In Is Real

this is what it means: filthy, impure, offensive. Well, that fits that devil rat exactly. Even just in the natural, a rat is filthy, impure, and offensive.

Heaven and Hell Are Real

Half a year after all this, I heard incredible stories of Mary K. Baxter who tells of how she has been in heaven many times and has seen different parts of hell. She said that there are huge rats weighing seventy-five pounds in hell and also big snakes. She has seen them there as well as all kinds of terrifying and offensive demons. Jesus took her to hell for her to see the horrors and the reality of it. But Jesus also brought her to heaven to see the glory and the beauty of heaven and things beyond this world, things we cannot even imagine. He showed her how real heaven and hell are, and told her that she must tell people all about it. You can see her on YouTube where she tells her story of what she had seen and what the Lord told her. Mary also has written books about it. She goes all over the world, and her ministry is to warn and tell the people where they will end up if they don't repent of their sin and don't make Jesus Lord of their lives. And if they do repent and live according to the Word of God, that there is a glorious Heaven waiting for them. Heaven is real and hell is real and the Word of God is real.

Ask the Lord if He will open up the eyes of your understanding so you can understand the Word of God. Many of us have read the Bible many times, and maybe you have even read it all of your life. Perhaps, to be honest, many times when you read the Bible, it doesn't say much to you anymore. If it is like that for you, ask the Lord for new insight and for a Spirit of wisdom and revelation for which Paul was praying in Colossians 1:9–10 and also in Ephesians 1:17.

You Are Putting Your Pain Above Me

Back to my story again. There was a night the pain was so bad that my husband and I both cried out to the Lord and asked, *"What are we doing wrong?"* The next day, early in the morning, while I was still in bed, I heard the Lord saying to me, *"You are putting your pain above Me."* I thought about it for a bit and said, "Yes, Lord, You are absolutely right." Right away I asked forgiveness and repented for putting my pain above the Lord. While I was repenting and placing Jesus above my pain, I felt a shift in my heart and started worshipping Jesus and told Him, "You are number one again in my life, *not* my pain."

In spite of the pain that was still there, I felt much better than before. Maybe it's strange to you, but I felt so blessed that Jesus told me what I was doing wrong. I understood at that moment that He was treating me as a daughter, like it says in Hebrews 12:5–7, as that word of encouragement that addresses you as sons":

> *"My son, do not make light of the Lord's discipline and do not lose heart when He rebukes you, because the Lord disciplines those He loves and He punishes everyone He accepts*

as a son. Endure hardship as discipline; God is treating you as sons.

And in verse 10-11 it says, *"but God disciplines us for our own good, that we may share in His holiness. No discipline seems pleasant at the time, but painful. Later on, however, it produces a harvest of righteousness and peace for those who have been trained by it."*

This was such an encouraging word for me because I felt so thankful and blessed that God was treating me as a daughter and was disciplining me for my good so that I may share in His holiness. It is not a pleasure when we are going through it, but praise God, it will bring forth a harvest of righteousness and peace, bringing you and me into the perfect place where the Lord has called us into. You may ask, "Did the pain go away after that?" No, it didn't, but I could handle it, knowing that the Lord was in all this and was training me and teaching me to live righteously by putting Him first in everything.

We don't hear much teaching about this, and I think it is because people don't really want to hear that at times we have to go through suffering to be purified so we can share in His holiness. In Hebrews 12:1–2 it says, *"Let us run with perseverance the race set before us. Let us fix our eyes on Jesus, the author and perfecter of our faith, Who, for the joy set before Him, endured the cross, scorning its shame, and sat down at the right hand of the throne of God."* We too can endure if we think about the joy that is set before us, for the glory that is waiting for us in heaven.

Every day with this excruciating pain was not easy. So I went to the doctor and asked something for the pain. The medication he gave me helped a little bit, but the side effect was that it made me dizzy, so I didn't take it regularly. There was one day, I was so dizzy on top of the pain, that I cried out to the Lord and rebuked the dizziness, but couldn't get my faith to work. We have a CD with healing scriptures, so that evening we both were listening to that CD over and over again. Even when we went to bed, we listened to it one more time. In the meantime, I was worshipping the Lord. Thank God, through His Word, the dizziness went away and I had a sound sleep.

Unclean, Unclean

Every day, I looked up scriptures about healing to keep up my faith and meditated on them. Also, I asked the Lord to open my eyes for the right scripture that would strengthen my faith. One morning, I was reading about the crucifixion, and, suddenly I realized that the Lord was made unclean with our sin—yes, with my sin—and I started to weep and weep intensely. I don't know how to describe it, but I felt so sad that the Lord had to become unclean and suffer so much humiliation for me because of my sin. Jesus, who is holy, blameless, and pure, was made unclean for me. Then my thoughts went out to the people with leprosy in the time of Jesus. Those people with leprosy had to cry out, *"Unclean, unclean,"* wherever they went so that the people around them would not come close to them and be contaminated.

That must have been so humiliating for those people to have to cry out "unclean". At that moment, I felt the humiliation those people had to go through because I imagined what it would have been like if I had to cry out "unclean, unclean," everywhere I went. Then I thought about what it must have been for Jesus when He was on the cross, hanging there naked with blood all over His body for everyone to see. They laughed and mocked and hurled insults at Him—all the humiliation, all the shame, and the unbearable pain he suffered. The only thing I could do at that moment was cry and weep for my Savior, whom I love so much. Through this, my love and appreciation grew still deeper for my Lord.

Remember, I asked the Lord to open my eyes for a scripture passage that would strengthen my faith. He did this in a special way, in a way I could not have come up with. The Lord is so good! I also knew that I was not unclean, even with all that stuff on my back, because Jesus had made me righteous and purified me through His blood.

It is wonderful when the Lord strengthens your faith, but I also learned to be careful with whom I could share what the Lord was doing in me. I went somewhere and talked to some sisters about what I was going through. Later when I came home, I felt so down, as if I lost my faith. I talked to the Lord about it because I didn't understand why I suddenly felt so down. The next morning, the Lord showed me a picture of a pot with a plant in it. The plant had been cut off, but there was a little side shoot growing right next to the cut-off plant. And the Lord said, "Your faith was crushed yesterday, but there is a new shoot of faith growing. *Water it with the Word.*" So I did. I read the Scriptures about healing again and drank from the water of the river of life through the Word. I let the Word of truth come into my heart, which strengthened my faith, and I felt so much better again.

By faith, we take what Jesus provides for us, and that is all the things we need for life and godliness through our knowledge of Him who called us by His own glory and goodness (see 2 Peter 1:3–4). We receive all those great and precious promises by faith in the Word, and through the knowledge of His Word. Because how can we have faith in the Word if we don't really have knowledge of the Word for ourselves? Don't go by what someone else tells you; dig into the Word for yourself so it becomes yours!!! I have experienced that big time because the words the Lord has revealed to me are now alive to me and are mine.

Chapter 11

Patience Is Very Important To The Lord

If the healing lingers, and we have examined ourselves, then we know the Lord is doing a deeper work in us and is changing things in us. There may be things inside of us that we don't even know are there until the Lord reveals them to us and deals with those issues. Other times, the Lord is simply testing our faith to see if we will hold onto Him and His Word. The process builds patience and endurance in us.

I found out through all I went through that patience is very important to the Lord. *Through standing in faith and waiting patiently, we receive our answers to prayer and the promises of the Word.* Also we receive through patience the personal promises the Lord has given to us. *Never give up.* The enemy wants us to give up in order for us to lose out. But the Lord always wants us to be blessed and healed (see 3 John 2). If we stand firm and hold on to the promises of the Word, we will never lose.

The Lord showed me in different ways how to receive His promises into my life. First of all, it is by faith. The faith that the Lord has given us is in our new born spirit, and when we learn to use our given faith we will become mature and strong in our faith. James 1:5–8 says it's clear that without faith we receive nothing. Faith gives us access to the will of God, which is His Word with all His promises. If we believe that the Word of God is the *absolute truth*, that the Word is given to us, and that His Word is His will for our lives, then it gives us security and we can settle His Word in our hearts. Then faith is not as difficult as we thought.

I love those verses in 1 John 5:14–15: *"This is the assurance we have in approaching God: that if we ask anything according to His will, He hears us. And if we know that He hears us—whatever we ask—we know that we have what we asked of Him."* This is what I would call *the law of faith*. We should never go back on our prayers when we know God has heard them. And yes, most of the time this requires patience. (I have a prayer going on with the Lord for a while now, but I know the Lord has heard me, and I will never back off. I will get the petition I desire of Him). When the Lord is testing our faith, our faith will develop and bring forth perseverance, and then we will receive (see James 1:3–4).

Oh my, believe it or not, while I'm writing this I sense a big smile on God's face because He loves to shower His blessings on us.

I Saw Myself with Our House Key in My Mouth

Once the Lord gave me a picture, and in that picture I saw myself with our house key in my mouth. I knew it was our house key because of the blue label that is on that key. The Lord made it clear to me that the authority He has given me in His Word is in my mouth. By speaking in authority and faith I receive the promises God has given me. I said, "Yes, I understand Lord, our house key opens the door to the entrance of the home that belongs to us. That means when I speak out your promises in faith, I have the entrance into your promises which are belonging to me, because you have given these promises to me already in your Word.

I understand from the Bible and realize there is also another side to speaking words out of our mouths. In Proverbs 6:2, it says that you can be ensnared by the words of your mouth. And in James 3:6, it says that the tongue is (can be) a fire, a world of evil among the parts of the body. It corrupts (can corrupt) the whole person and set the whole course of his life on fire and is itself set on fire by hell.

I put the "can be" in parentheses because we don't have to speak bad things; we don't have to speak curses. The better way is that we speak good things and blessings, then good things will be coming our way.

"The tongue has the power of life and death, and those who love it will eat its fruit" (Prov. 18:21). When we speak good things and blessings, we will reap good things and blessings, and when we speak bad things and curses in our lives or over the lives of others, we will reap bad things and the curses we speak. In Galatians 6:7-8 it says it very strongly too: *"Do not be deceived, God cannot be mocked. A man reaps what he sows. The one who sows to please his sinful nature, from that nature will reap destruction; the one who sows to please the Spirit, from the Spirit will reap eternal life."*

By speaking from our carnal nature, we give the enemy a foothold in our lives or in the situation we are in (Eph. 4:27). However, when we speak in faith the promises of God's Word, the law of the Spirit of life in Christ Jesus will come to action and set us free from the law of sin and death. This is according to Romans 8:2. By speaking the Word, His promises, which are God's will, will set us free from the forces of darkness. It will set us free from sickness and disease or whatever binds us so we can be free to serve the Lord in every way and live in newness of life (see Rom. 6:4).

The essence of dying to ourselves is always in the picture as it says in Romans 6:11–12: *"In the same way, count yourselves dead to sin (*sickness*), but alive to God in Christ Jesus. Therefore do not let sin* (sickness*) reign in your mortal body so that you obey its evil desires."* And I say amen to that; I am not a slave to the enemy anymore! This is true because Christ Jesus has made me free from the law of sin and death (sickness). I put sickness in brackets because sin and sickness are a package deal.

That morning, when the Lord spoke to me through those scriptures, His word rose up in me: "The reality is found in Christ." Those words touched me, and I looked it up in the Word of God; this is what it says in Colossians

2:17: *"These are a shadow of the things that were to come; the reality, however, is found in Christ."* At that, I yelled out: *"I belong to Christ! I triumph over every sickness, pain, and also over this devil rat because of Christ. He triumphed, and in Christ, I triumph! On Christ the solid rock I stand, all other ground is sinking sand."* The Word of God is for me God's heart and such a reality; it is solid for me. Everything evolves in Christ. In Ephesians 4:10, it says that Christ fills the whole universe, and in Hebrews 1:3, it says that the Son sustains all things by His powerful Word.

I wept as peace came into my heart, and I said, "Thank you, Lord, I am an overcomer by Your blood and the testimony of Your Word" (Rev. 12:11). After that, I decided not to take any of those pills for the pain anymore. I stood in faith in what the Lord had shown me through His Word. I didn't want to take those pills anyway because of the side effects. They made me dizzy, and on top of it, I was unable to focus clearly anymore. I didn't like that at all—it even scared me because I didn't want to lose my vision in any way.

The Truth Of The Word Has To Be Rooted In Us

The next morning, my back was burning more and was redder than the days before, but my decision was made and that was that. No more pills! *I trust you, Lord, completely.* How could I not trust Him, knowing all He had done for me and His having revealed so much about the Scriptures to me? I started meditating again on Romans 6:4,

11-12 as well as chapter 8:2, and Colossians 2:17. I learned during these times that, yes, we can be touched by the Lord through the Word, but healing is not always instant or the way we expect it to be. Sometimes the truth of the Word has to be rooted in us first before the healing can take place.

I decided to hold onto my spoken word of faith. I did not want to lose what the Lord had done the day before, that the reality of my healing is found in Christ alone. Hebrews 11:11 encouraged me a lot because I saw Abraham's trust in the Lord which enabled him to become a Father. He considered God faithful who made the promise. Also in Romans 4:20 I saw that Abraham did not waver at the promise of God through unbelief, but was strong in faith as he gave glory to God. Abraham was fully persuaded that what God had promised, He is also able to perform.

One night, when my husband and I were praying, the Lord said to me, *"My blood is the guarantee for your healing and the fulfillment of all My promises."* When I heard those words, it almost took my breath away. I had been in awe of the Lord for quite some time. I could hardly believe that the Lord said that to me. Yes, He said it to me! What a loving and kind God we serve that He wants to speak to us, and yes, of course, He wants to speak to us—we are His children. How encouraging!!! Think about it, the blood that flowed out of the wounds of Jesus is the guarantee for our healing.

Also, the Lord said to my husband, "Faith is a law and is set in motion by your speaking and acting upon it." That confirmed to me the picture the Lord gave me when I saw myself with our house key in my mouth. The key is our authority; through speaking and declaring in faith our desire, we receive. We also see this clearly in Mark 11:22–24: *"Have faith in God, Jesus answered. I tell you the truth, if anyone says to this mountain go throw yourself into the sea and does not doubt in his heart but believes that those things which he said shall come to pass; he shall have whatever he said. Therefore I tell you whatever you ask for in prayer, belief, imagine that you have received it and it will be yours."*

Those are powerful words, and it is good to meditate on them and ask the Lord to bring revelation to us in order that they may become alive to us and we can live by faith. That is what God desires for us. He says, "My righteous shall live by faith." There is another very familiar Scripture in Matthew 18:19 that states: *"Again I tell you that if two of you on earth agree about anything you ask for, it shall be done for you by my Father in heaven."* One morning when I was reading this, the words "*it shall*" really struck me, and I said out loud, *"It shall, it shall, it shall be done for me by my Father."* This word *shall* is a strong word; it cannot be said any stronger. This is the law of faith. Jesus is telling us that if we have faith and agree together on earth for something, it *shall* be done by my Father in heaven. We ask on earth and the Father in heaven *shall* answer our prayers.

Again, we have to meditate on these words in the presence of God so they will become real to us. Hear me, I am not saying that whatever you ask will be presented to you right away. No, most of the time it takes some time. The Lord knows exactly when we are ready for it, and sometimes He has to prepare even other people to cooperate with Him for a certain situation. Another important aspect is that our desire has to be in line with the Lord and His Word. In John 15:7, Jesus said, *"If you remain in me and my words remain in you, ask whatever you wish and it shall be given to you."* Here we see how important it is for our faith to stay alive and that we remain in Jesus—and that His words remain in us.

As Christians, we can sometimes slack off in reading God's Word on a daily basis. If we don't read our Bible every day and live humbly and stay in tune with the Lord, it becomes difficult to live in faith and receive from the Lord. But we don't have to stay that way; if we cry out to the Lord, He is faithful and will show us the way to come close to Him again.

Lord There Must Be a Way Out—For You Are the Way

A while ago, the Lord gave me a vision. I saw people on a seashore. Huge waves were coming my way, then I saw a man coming out of one of those waves and he was thrown onto the sand. It took a while before he got his breath back and could stand up again. Then suddenly, I was surrounded by all of those huge waves, and the only thing I could see was water all around me, water under me, and water on top of me. Then I cried out to the Lord: *"Lord, there must be a way out, for You are the Way. There must be a way out! Where is the way?"* Suddenly, I was taken up and stood on top of all that water. What an experience! After that I questioned the Lord: "Lord, I know you are the Way, but what are you showing me? What is the meaning of those people in this vision, and what about that man who came out of the waves and was thrown onto the sand?"

This is the impression the Lord gave me: *Because you know My way, tell My people that there is always, always a way out of their overwhelming situations, whether out of sickness, out of darkness, or out of pain. Through Me, all things are possible for those who cry out to Me and Me only, for those who put their trust in Me and Me only. The man is a picture of the people who are pushed out of the wild waves of this world and are coming into My rest. There is still a little time for them to come in. I am coming soon, so they need to be taught My ways. Without Me, there is no Truth and without the Truth, there is no Life. I am the only way out! The truth of My way needs to be explained well, in order for My children to enter and live forever in the kingdom of My Father. Nobody can come to the Father except through Me!*

When I was meditating and praying about this, I heard the Lord say, "the knowledge of the truth." Then there was a pause, and I saw a door going open. The Lord continued, "The knowledge of the truth opens the door to My kingdom."

My response was, yes, the Gospel needs to be explained clearly, for Jesus is the only way to come into the kingdom of the Father. There are many people and even pastors who are saying that there are many ways to enter heaven, but the Bible is very clear about this. Look at 1 Timothy 2:4–5: *"God wants all men to be saved and to come to the knowledge of the truth. For there is one God and one mediator between*

God and man, the Man Christ Jesus, who gave Himself as a ransom for all men." The knowledge of the truth is this: *the Man Christ Jesus who gave Himself up for all of us, He is the only way because He is the one mediator between God and men.* Here we see that God the Father loves us so much that He gave His one and only Son that whoever believes in Him shall not perish but have eternal life.

When we accept Jesus as our Lord and Savior, then God becomes our Father instead of God being a consuming fire. Yes, God is to be feared because He is the one who can cause us to land in the fires of hell, if we keep ignoring Him and rebel at the great salvation Jesus has prepared for us. The knowledge of the truth of the God/Man Christ Jesus opens the door for us to the kingdom of the Father forever. Titus 1:1–2 says that *the knowledge of the truth leads to godliness—a faith and knowledge resting on the hope of eternal life, which God, who does not lie, promised before the beginning of time.*

The knowledge of the truth opens the small gate to eternal life, and as we walk the narrow road, we should reflect the kingdom of God to the world around us. We have to let our lives shine and display to the world who Jesus is. "For we are His workmanship to fulfill His plan and walk the paths which He prepared for us to go" (see Eph. 2:10).

Consider It Pure Joy

It took about five months before I was healed of shingles. And even months after that I had to rebuke some of the pain symptoms I felt again, in order for it not to come back. It was not a spectacular healing this time, but I am very thankful to the Lord for the things He taught me through the process of healing as well as the revelations the Lord gave me of certain scriptures about faith. I'm also thankful that I was able in the midst of excruciating pain, to make Jesus Lord of that pain and cry out with Psalm 22:3 that pain or no pain; *"You O God, are enthroned as the Holy One, You are my praise and in You, I put my trust."*

I learned from this to make Jesus Lord of everything in every situation of my life. It gave and gives me security. Also, I started to appreciate James 1:2–4, 12, and see things with an eternal perspective—the way God sees it:

> *Consider it pure joy, my brothers, whenever you face trials of many kinds because you know that the testing of your faith develops perseverance. Perseverance must finish its work so that you may be mature and complete, not lacking anything. ...Blessed is the man who perseveres under trial because when he has stood the test, he will receive the victors crown of life that God has promised to those who love Him.*

Author's Note and Prayer

The lessons the Lord gives us sometimes are not always the easiest, and I must say they are difficult most of the time. Yet it is our attitude and knowing the Word that makes all the difference on how we come through those hard times. When we hold on to His precious promises, we will come out victorious. Remember that we are God's treasure—yes, His trophy!!!

Father, how glorious is your plan of salvation because from the beginning on You knew that we would blow it on all sides, and You already prepared a way out of all our trouble through Your Son, Jesus Christ, who became our Savior forevermore.

Therefore, my Father, I intercede for Your children in the mighty name of Jesus, for understanding and open eyes to the spiritual warfare they are in right now and to see their way out of their pain and trouble. Yes to see the way You have already prepared for them in your foreknowledge. Open their eyes to dreams and visions to see what is hidden for them at the moment, in order to understand your plan in their lives. Father, You are enthroned as the Holy One, therefore, enable your people to place You above everything and make You number one in any situation. Lift them up with your righteous right hand, and set them on top of the wild waters of this world.

Patience Is Very Important To The Lord

Father, I pray for their strength and perseverance to hold on to your plan and to see the way out and the deliverance they are longing for. Thank You, Lord, for your goodness and answering my prayer in Jesus' name, amen.

Part 5:
The Bride Of Christ

Chapter 12

My Longing For Jesus

What I am about to write in this last part is most precious to me. We, as born-again Christians, belong to the bride of Jesus Christ, the lover of our soul. Paul says in Philippians 3:13-14 *"Forgetting what is behind and straining toward what is ahead. I press on toward the coal to win the prize for which God has called me heavenward in Christ Jesus."* To me this is the "high calling of God" being the bride of Jesus; there is no higher calling on earth than this call—to belong to the bride of Christ.

In 1997, we participated in a forty-day fast at our church, and during that time, one morning, when I was praying, I saw a vision. In that vision, I saw the Lord giving me a wedding gown. It was for me and my husband, and my first thought was, we cannot fit together in one dress. And the Lord responded to my thoughts and said, *"You both belong to the bride."* O my, what a joy flooded my soul in a deep longing for Jesus.

Then ten days later during the worship in a Sunday morning service, I saw myself in this wedding gown, walking toward the Lord Jesus. It was in a huge room or space, and I saw Jesus in a distance. He was waiting for me. I couldn't see His face, but I knew it was Jesus, His whole being was light. Again a deep longing rose up in me for Jesus, a longing to see him and to be with the One I love so much. I started weeping.

That Sunday night, I was awakened, and my thoughts went to what I saw that morning in the worship service, and again my heart longed for the lover of my soul. While I was lying in bed, reveling in Jesus' love, I repeatedly said to my Lord: "Purify me, make me holy, make me like gold, pure gold, and set me apart ready to do Your will. Let Your kingdom flood my soul." What an amazing time I had with my loving Lord! His presence was so awesome and lasted for a long time. Belonging to the bride of Jesus is so real for me and most precious!!!

I like to share some Scriptures the Lord has shown me in connection with the bride.

Song of Songs

There is a whole book in the Bible dedicated to the bride, called "Song of Songs." I absolutely love it and have read it many times, though I must say, I don't understand everything. But what the Lord has taught me, I will tell you, and I pray that you will get as excited as I am about being a part of His bride. The Song of Songs is also called Songs of Solomon. The view of the Song is an allegory of the love relationship between God and Israel. Solomon is identified with God and the Shulamite with Israel. This is in view with the Old Testament and typifies God's love for Israel.

In the New Testament, Solomon is identified by Jesus' relationship with the true church, which is His bride.

Jesus Gave His Blood as a Dowry for His Bride.

The love Jesus has for his bride is astonishing. Think with me about the price Jesus had to pay for us, his bride. The Father required Jesus, his Son, to shed his blood for the forgiveness and cleansing of our sins, in order to receive us as a pure bride, without spot or wrinkle. This was the requirement the Father asked of Jesus in order for us to be his glorious bride and to be on his side for all eternity!!!

On this requirement of the blood, the Lord gave me a vision. One morning around Easter time when I was still in bed, I was thinking about the resurrection of Jesus and His ascension to heaven to His Father. I thought that must have been spectacular after the greatest victory of mankind over the devil and his angels. My thought was that the angels of God and the entire heavenly host must have been thrilled to hear about that victory, and that all those angels would have been shouting hallelujah. I imagined hallelujahs all over heaven and glory flashing all around Him by welcoming Jesus back into heaven.

But no, I was surprised that the Lord corrected me on Jesus' spectacular home coming in heaven with this vision. I saw Jesus going to His Father and kneeling before Him. In His hands, He had His own blood for the forgiveness of mankind, lost in sin and death, and the Father accepted the blood of Jesus for our forgiveness. When I saw Jesus bow down before His Father with His blood, there was total silence in heaven; *it was an absolutely holy moment.* That's the only way I can describe it. No flashing glory, no shouting, nothing of that all; ***there was a holy silence!***

Many impressions came to my mind with this vision. Jesus, the Son of God, became a servant (see Phil. 2:7). The Son of Man obeyed His Father in shedding His blood and brought it to Him as a servant, in humility, kneeling before Him saying, "Father, I did what You asked me to do. This is My blood for the forgiveness of your people (see Heb. 9:24–26). The Father accepted His blood and established Jesus again as His Son, as it says in Hebrews 1:5 (AMP): *"I have begotten You, established You in an official Sonship relation, with kingly dignity. And again, I will be to Him a Father, and He will be to Me a Son."* By the acceptance of the blood of Jesus, Jesus was established again as His Son, and we now could become the bride of Christ.

This is what Jesus told His disciples before He went to the cross, as it is written in John 14:1–3:

> *Do not let your heart be troubled. Trust in God, trust also in Me. In My Father's house are many rooms, if it were not so, I would have told you. And if I go and prepare a place for you, I will come back and take you to be with Me that you also may be where I am.*

Here we see that after Jesus' death and resurrection, He went to heaven to his Father to prepare a place for His bride.

Jesus knew all along that through shedding His blood, He would betroth us as His bride.

Jesus left this earth knowing that He would come back a second time but as Bridegroom to take us as His bride to be with Him forever. Hallelujah! The disciples didn't understand this at that time. We can read the letters of the apostle Paul, where we see that he had received revelation from the Lord about His return, and that he teaches us to expect Jesus at any time and to be ready for His coming (see 1 Thes.4:13–17).

The Purity of the Bride Is Required in the Bible

The requirement that the Lord gives for His bride is to be absolutely pure, totally dedicated to Him in love, honor, and respect. Jesus should be number one in all we do because we cannot serve two masters as it says in Matthew 6:24. There can be only one person in our lives who can be number one, and the Lord is asking and expecting from us that He is that number one!!!

The Bible requires an extremely high standard of purity. We can absolutely live up to that high standard when we are dedicated, knowing how much Jesus loves us and about the glory that is waiting for us in heaven. When we know in our hearts His deep love and desire for us, and know how He sees us as His beautiful bride, then it's a joy to reach out to our Lover and put Him first in everything we do.

Look what it says in the Song of Songs 2:13–15: *"Arise, my love, my beautiful one, and come with Me."* The Amplified Bible says:

> *So I went with Him and when we were climbing the rocky steps up the hillside, my beloved Shepherd said to me, O my dove, while you are here in the seclusion of the cleft of the solid rock, in the sheltered and secret place of the cleft, let Me see your face, let Me hear your voice; for your voice is sweet and your face is lovely. My heart was touched and I fervently sang to Him my desire. Take for us the foxes, the little foxes that spoil the vineyards of our love, for our vineyards are in blossom.* (Song of Songs 2:14-15 AMP)

I love those couple of verses because we can see in those verses Jesus' desire for us to spend time with Him. Most of the time in the Bible it will say, "Come to Me," but here Jesus is saying, *"Come with Me."* This tells me that He wants real fellowship with us while we are climbing those rocky steps of life up to the hill. He wants to be there with us when the way is rocky and difficult because those rocky steps are too hard and difficult to climb by ourselves. Our Christian walk is not always easy, and sometimes it is downright difficult. We have to lay down our own will in order to please the Lord and do His will.

My Longing For Jesus

We have to hear with the ears of our hearts what our Bridegroom, our Lover, is saying: "*O my dove, while you are here in the seclusion of the cleft*—in your special place at home and your set-apart time—*let Me see your face, and let Me hear your voice, for your voice is sweet and your face is lovely.*" (Song of Songs 2:14)

Jesus is telling us here in the Song of Songs that our face is lovely and our voice is sweet; He admires our faces and loves to hear our voices. Jesus loves to hear us praying and praising Him, He loves to hear our singing, and He loves it when we cry out to Him and pour out our hearts before Him. Yes, it touches Jesus' heart when we spend our time with Him and when we reach out to Him with our whole heart. Through it, Jesus will touch our hearts as it says in Song of Songs 2:15 (this quotation is in my own words) My heart was touched, and I fervently sang to Him my desire. Then she cries out to the Lord, "O God take away the foxes that—take away that sin that spoils our relationship of love and forgive those little sins that are holding me back from coming into full bloom and intimacy with You."

Then there is another cry: *"My beloved is mine and I am His!"* (Song of Songs 2:16) How beautiful is it when we ourselves can cry out those words from our hearts? *My beloved is mine and I am His!*

Jesus' Desire Is For Us, His Bride

A while ago, I saw in a vision some rocks, and I saw an open space in the middle of one of those rocks. Light shone out of that open space, and I sensed the Lord saying to me, *"Come with Me to that secret place and spend time with Me alone."* The Lord desires this for all of us who are His bride, not just for me or a few of us. He desires that intimate relationship with all of us, His bride. He wants to bestow His love on us. He wants us to enjoy Him and relex in His presence. And in the time we are fellowshipping with the Lord, He is able to do a sanctifying work in us. In this way, we will become totally free in our ability to express our love and adoration for Him. He can unlock the well of living water in us so that we can pour out His love, His life, yes, His blessing on others who are in desperate need of that pure love. Many are in need of real love because so many have never experienced that pure love nor do they know about eternal life and blessings untold.

Also, in our relationship with the Lord and the sanctifying work He is doing in us, we are also preparing ourselves for the coming of our Bridegroom in the air.

To become free in our relationship with Jesus is a process, and through that process, it gives us much peace and joy in our hearts. It makes us secure in trusting Jesus and trusting and knowing His love and goodness for us.

A Bit about My Journey of Purity

To come back to where I was talking about our purity as the bride of Jesus, I'd like to tell you about some of my journeys in this. My husband had prayed to God for a girl who would be his wife and would be fitted for him. The Lord

My Longing For Jesus

brought me into his life; we fell in love and got married. At that time, I was not saved, I didn't know the Lord, and I was deeply wounded. Because of my wounds, I couldn't get that oneness with my husband where my heart was longing for. When we both surrendered our lives to the Lord, it brought a big change in me, and it also brought the healing that I so desperately needed. Through the years I began to understand the importance of being pure and to live pure and holy before each other. But also to live pure and holy before the Lord in order to become one with Him and each other. Because of my longing to be one with the Lord and my husband, I totally gave myself up.

One Sunday night, we had a special service at our church, and at the last song, before the altar call, I knelt down at the place where we were sitting and said to the Lord, "Take my body. I give my body to you." Then the Lord touched me deeply at that moment, and I started crying. I said again and again, "I give my body to You." By then I was sobbing fully, "Lord, my body was misused for somebody's pleasure, but now, my Jesus, I sacrifice my body to You. Use me for Your glory!"

When I spoke that out, I began to be afraid and said to my husband, "I need help, please pray for me. This is so deep, please help me." He didn't hear me because of the volume of the music, and he had no idea what was going on in me. But he put his hand on me and prayed, and the Lord helped me in my deep despair because *He is the only one who can help and set our soul free and purify us from abuse.*

We Are Trophies Of Christ's Victory

> The next day, I read in Romans 12:1-2 *"Therefore I urge you, brothers, in the view of God's mercy, to offer your bodies as living sacrifices, holy and pleasing to God which is your spiritual worship. Do not conform any longer to the pattern of this world, but be transformed by the renewing of your mind. Then you will be able to test and approve what God's will is His good, pleasing and perfect will."*

When I read that scripture I was amazed because without knowing it at the time, that was exactly what I had done the night before in the church. I gave my body as a living sacrifice to Him. And again I said to the Lord; "Here I am, If there is anything more necessary you need to do in me, go ahead and make me pure without any spot or wrinkle." At that moment, the presence of the Holy Spirit was very real and beautiful, and with my whole heart I longed even more for my Lord, my Jesus, the Lover of my soul.

I began to understand why it is very important to be a pure virgin before marriage. I had never felt so pure, and at the same time when I felt so pure, I saw a clear picture of a beautiful, fresh, red cherry. I said to the Lord, "What is the meaning Lord, of this beautiful cherry you are showing me?" I had no idea what it meant; therefore, I went to the computer and googled the word, *cherry*. I was so surprised by what I saw that I almost fell off my chair. Because the first thing Google returned when I searched for the meaning of the word 'cherry' were the words; *virginity* and *virgin*. Also it said as an example: *"I am eighteen and still have my cherry."*

Well, this blew my mind because I had asked the Lord to confirm to me that I was a pure virgin in His sight. And I had never heard that expression such as *I am eighteen and still have my cherry*. The Lord confirmed this in such a way that I could not muster up any doubt or unbelief. I understood at that moment how the Lord desires for a couple to go into marriage, pure and with a deep longing for each other. If every couple would start a marriage in that way, I suppose there would be fewer problems in marriages. But thank God for His grace; that He is always there to help us, to heal us, and purify us from our wounded pasts. *Yes, He has redeemed our past*. Hallelujah, I'm so thankful!

What Is the Symbol of a Dove in Song of Songs?

Now years later, writing this part of the book about the bride, I asked the Lord what it means in the book of Song of Songs where He says, "*Your eyes are doves*" or just the word "*my dove.*" What is the symbol of a dove in Song of Songs? I was really curious about this because shortly after becoming born again, my husband started calling me "my dove" or "my dovie," not knowing that this was written in the book of Song of Songs.

Yes, we all know that the dove symbolizes the Holy Spirit in the Bible. In the gospels when Jesus was baptized and came up out of the water, the heavens opened and the Spirit of God descended on Jesus in the form of a dove. But I thought that in Song of Songs it must symbolize something else, so I asked the Lord about it, and He replied to me saying, *"In the Song of Songs, the dove symbolizes purity."* So I looked up those scriptures in Song of Songs again and thought, *Oh yes, of course, that makes sense because the Lord is calling on His bride, His pure bride!* As it says in Song of Songs 5:2, "My darling, My dove, My flawless one," and also in 6:9, "My dove, my undefiled and perfect one." Yes, the Lord is coming for a bride who is pure, flawless, and without spot or wrinkle.

In 2 Corinthians 11:2, Paul says, *"For I am jealous for you with godly jealousy. I promised you to one husband, to Christ, so that I might present you as a pure virgin to Him."* The Lord has given a new spirit to live in us, a spirit that is totally pure and righteous. Therefore the Lord expects from us to walk in purity and righteousness. That is why He gave us His Word to live by and His commands to keep as He explains in John 14:15, *"If you love Me, you will obey what I command,"* and in verse 23, *"If anyone loves Me, He will obey My teaching."*

When you love someone, you want to please that person right? So it is with our Lord. We love Him; therefore, we want to please Him with all our hearts and do what He asks us to do, just as He loves us and bestows His love and goodness upon us.

Chapter 13

A Humble, A Longing, And An Expecting Heart

The next point I would like to mention concerns the humility we should see in the bride of Christ. In Song of Songs 2:1 (AMP this refers to the beloved) *She said, "I am only a little rose or an autumn crocus of the plain of Sharon, or a humble lily of the valleys that grows in deep and difficult places."* Then look at what our Lover's response is in the next verse: *"Like a lily among thorns, so are you, my love, among the daughters."* I love how Jesus reacts when we humble ourselves, He always will lift us up and give us grace!!!

We see this also in the book of Ruth. *The book of Ruth is a prophetic picture of the bride.* We see the humility of Ruth when she lays down at the feet of Boaz and asks him to spread the corner of his garment to cover her because he was her kinsman-redeemer. He did redeem her, and she became his bride. (See Ruth 3 and 4.) One morning, still in bed, I was thinking about how Ruth was laying at the feet of Boaz, and my thoughts were: *That is our place as Christians, as the bride of Christ, lying at the feet of Jesus, humbly awaiting a sign of the Master.* At that moment, I saw a vision where I was lying at the threshing-floor with my Redeemer, and suddenly tears were streaming from my eyes. It was a precious moment with the Lord who was confirming the thoughts I just had about the humility of the bride of Christ.

In Luke 7:37-38, we see another woman who completely humbled herself in repentance at the feet of Jesus. She stood behind Him at His feet, weeping, as she began to wet His feet with her tears. Then she wiped His feet with her hair, kissed His feet, and poured perfume on them.

We also see in Luke 10:38-41, Mary, the sister of Martha humbly sitting at Jesus' feet listening to what He was saying. Martha was busy and distracted by all the preparations that had to be made, but Mary was listening intently to the Lord. *Nothing was more important to her than listening to the voice of Jesus.* Martha got upset with Mary, and listen to what Jesus said about this: *"Mary has chosen what is better and it will not be taken away from her."*

Because of Mary's humility and her love for the Lord and having been listening to Him with her whole heart, we see that she understood what was about to happen to Jesus. She took an alabaster jar of very expensive perfume and poured it on Jesus' head as He was reclining at the table. The disciples had no idea what she was doing and thought that it was a waste. They were even indignant and said, "This perfume could have been sold at a high price and the money given to the poor." But Jesus came to her defense as we can read in Matthew 26:6–14. Aware of this, Jesus said to them:

Why are you bothering this woman? She has done a beautiful thing to Me. The poor you will always have with you but you will not always have Me. When she poured the perfume on My body she did it to prepare Me for burial. I tell you the truth, wherever this Gospel is preached throughout the world, what she has done to Me will also be told in memory of her.

Look at the love of Jesus at this moment. He was honoring Mary while He knew the horrible suffering that was soon coming upon Him. Jesus blessed her heart for the deep love she had for Him.

This should encourage all of us who live humbly with a deep love and hunger for the Lord. *When we are in heaven, we will be honored for the things we have done on earth, even for things we never realized had impacted our Savior's heart.*

A Longing Heart For Our Bridegroom.

There is another characteristic of the bride, and that is a longing heart for her Bridegroom. We see this very clearly in Mary Magdala in John 20:10–16:

Then the disciples went back to their homes, but Mary stood outside of the tomb crying. As she wept, she bent over to look into the tomb and saw two angels in white seated where

We Are Trophies Of Christ's Victory

Jesus' body had been, one at the head and the other at the foot. They asked her, "Woman why are you crying?" "They have taken my Lord away," she said, "and I don't know where they have put him."

At this, she turned around and saw Jesus standing there, but she did not realize that it was Jesus. Woman, He said why are you crying? Who is it you are looking for? Thinking he was the gardener she said, Sir, if You have carried Him away tell me where you have put Him and I will get Him." Jesus said to her, "Mary."

At the moment Jesus said to her, "Mary," she knew instantly who He was.

Jesus revealed Himself at the longing of her heart. Mary's tears were showing the longing and love she had for Jesus. The disciples went back home, but Mary couldn't leave. She stood outside the tomb weeping for Jesus. To her, the death of Jesus was horrible, but the empty tomb was unbearable. She had to find the one whom her soul loved, as it says in the Song of Songs 3:3,-4.

Love is the highest and most powerful law of the Kingdom of God. Mary's love and longing heart for Jesus compelled Him to go to her and reveal Himself even before He went to His Father in heaven. The instant Mary knew that it was her Lord, she clung to Him, but Jesus said, *"Do not hold on to Me, for I have not yet returned to the Father. Go instead to my brothers and tell them, I am returning to My Father and your Father, to, My God and your God"* (John 20:17).

Now we, who have experienced the new birth and know that God is our Father through our Lord Jesus, we know through the Spirit also that He is coming for a bride, a virgin who is pure and ready, waiting and expecting her Bridegroom.

Waiting and Expecting Our Bridegroom

Waiting and expecting our Bridegroom is the next point I want to make because the Bible is very clear that not all of the virgins will go up in the rapture, as we see in the parable of the ten virgins in Matthew 25:1–13:

> *At that time the Kingdom of heaven will be like ten virgins who took their lamps and went out to meet the bridegroom. Five of them were foolish and five were wise. The foolish ones took their lamps but did not take any oil with them. The wise, however, took oil in jars along with their lamps. The bridegroom was a long time in coming, and they all became drowsy and fell asleep.*
>
> *At midnight the cry rang out; Here is the bridegroom! Come out to meet him!*

Then all the virgins woke up and trimmed their lamps. The foolish ones said to the wise, give us some of your oil, our lamps are going out. No, they replied, there may not be enough for both us and you. Instead, go to those who sell oil and buy some for yourselves.

But while they were on their way to buy the oil, the bridegroom arrived. The virgins who were ready went in with him to the banquet. And the door was shut. Later the others also came. Sir! Sir! they said, open the door for us. But he replied, I tell you the truth, I don't know you. Therefore keep watch, because you do not know the day or the hour.

This is a very important piece of scripture if your desire is to be one of the wise virgins—if your desire is to go up in the rapture to meet the Lord Jesus in the air and be a part of the wedding banquet.

One night, when we were praying, the Lord gave me this word: "In heaven, everything is prepared and geared up for the bride to come home, but the bride seems to prepare herself to stay on the earth. She is making sure that she has everything she needs to stay alive when troubles come on the earth." Then there was a little pause before the Lord continued, and He said strongly, *"Not so! You prepare yourself in order to be ready to go up to Me, Your Bridegroom, because the time is short."* This shocked me, but yes, I could very well see

A Humble, A Longing, And An Expecting Heart

what the Lord was saying to me. Because many Christians are stacking up dried food and also water in making sure that they have everything when the tribulation comes, they don't really believe that the Lord is coming for them. After this word I was concerned about it and went looking for scriptures about *"being ready"* and *"preparing yourself for the trumpet call of God."*

In the parable of the ten virgins, we see that five were foolish and five were wise. The foolish ones went out and only took their lamps. But the wise prepared themselves in taking along with their lamps a jar of oil in case the bridegroom was a long time coming. I will try to explain what I understand from the Word of God about the meaning or the significance of the words; *lamp, oil, preparation, foolish,* and *wise*. With regard to the story of the virgins, most of the time we only hear about the oil of being filled with the Holy Spirit, but there is much more to it than just the oil. Yes, the oil represents the Holy Spirit, but there is also a lamp and preparation.

In Psalm 119:105, we see that the Word is a lamp to our feet and a light for our path. Also, in 2 Peter 1:19 it says, *"And we have the Word of the prophets made more certain, and you will do well to pay attention to it as to a light shining in a dark place, until the day dawns and the morning star rises in your hearts."* When we pay attention to the Word and its teachings and commands, keeping them in our hearts, it will do its work in us, as it is written in Proverbs 6:20–23. When I was reading that passage one day, I was amazed about this because it is so true and I have experienced it in different ways. It says: *"When you walk, they will guide you; when you sleep, they will watch over you; when you are awake, they will speak to you. For their commands are a lamp, this teaching is a light, and corrections of discipline are the way to live."* Here we see when we obey and live in accordance with the Word of God, the Word together with the Holy Spirit will purify and prepare us for Jesus' coming.

Revelation 19:7-8 says: *"Let us rejoice and be glad and give Him glory! For the wedding of the Lamb has come, and his bride has made herself ready. Fine linen, bright and clean was given her to wear." (Fine linen stands for the righteous acts of the saints.)* Here we see that we have something to do to be ready. The verse clearly says His bride has made herself ready. This means in a practical way that we have to live righteously and pure or we can forget our rapture and stay behind like a foolish virgin. I surely don't want to stay here on earth and end up in the great tribulation. And I don't want that for you, either. I am praying for all of you who are reading this book to be ready for His coming in Jesus' name, amen.

The Wise and Foolish Builders

There is another scripture that is very clear about this in Matthew 7:24-27. Jesus is talking about the wise and foolish builders. He says:

A Humble, A Longing, And An Expecting Heart

> *Therefore everyone who hears these words of mine and puts them into practice is like a wise man who built his house on the rock.*
>
> *The rain came down, the streams rose, and the winds blew and beat against that house, yet it did not fall, because it had its foundation on the rock. But everyone who hears these words of Mine and does not put them into practice is like a foolish man who built his house on sand. The rain came down, the streams rose, and the winds blew and beat against that house, and it fell with a great crash.*

Our Lord uses words that are very clear so we don't misunderstand them. We won't have any excuse and say, "Well, I didn't know that was in the Bible."

In verse 21, prior to this, Jesus said, *"Not everyone who says to Me, Lord, Lord, will enter the Kingdom of heaven, but only he who does the will of My Father who is in heaven."* Jesus speaks very clearly here so we can understand what He is saying. Yes, Jesus is sharp in how He put things, even to the point that He said to His disciples—'You do not want to leave too, do you?' (Because many took offense at what Jesus was saying at that time and many left Him.) *Simon Peter answered Him, "Lord to whom shall we go? You have the words of eternal life. We believe and know that You are the Holy One of God."* (See John 6:67-69). Neither Jesus nor

His Word ever changes; Jesus is always the same yesterday, today, and forever!

The Oil That Keeps Us Burning

In obeying His teaching, we weave, as it were, our wedding garment. Isn't that cool? The Word always fires me up and keeps me burning through the power of the Holy Spirit. The Holy Spirit which represents the oil in the parable of the wise and foolish virgins. The oil, the Holy Spirit, is very important because without the oil, without the Holy Spirit, there is no light. Without the oil, without the Holy Spirit, there is no understanding of the Word, no revelation of the Word, resulting in the inability to see the seriousness of the Word.

From 1 Peter 2:7-8, we come to understand that Jesus is our Rock or Stone that the builders rejected and became the capstone; also that He is a stone that causes men to stumble and a rock that makes them fall.

When we understand, through the Holy Spirit, how incredibly important it is to take the Word of God seriously, then we take the Bible and look to it as a light in the darkness—we do what it says and receive what God's intention is for us. Then we will know that the Lord's incredible love is never-ending, and His glory is always increasing. We will go from glory to glory, throughout eternity, as the bride of Jesus.

Oil also represents the presence of the Holy Spirit. It is the oil that keeps a lamp burning. Oil in the natural world needs to be purchased; it costs us something, right? *This is also in the spiritual—to have the presence of God continually in our lives costs us something.* There is a price to be paid, the giving up of our lives and our own desires, the price of spending time at the feet of Jesus in order to get to know Him and His Word. By doing this, we can keep the fire burning throughout the storms of life. It keeps us standing strong and firm on the rock in dark nights that may come our way.

This also means that our preparation at the feet of Jesus cannot be transferred or shared, as some of those virgins wanted to do in the parable of the wise and foolish virgins. *Preparation is a personal matter.* It is building our own relationship and being close to Jesus for ourselves. We can't afford to be lukewarm and live for ourselves and our own pleasures all the time because we cannot get our spiritual life in order at the last moment. *When the trumpet call comes, we have to be ready!!!*

Eagerly Desire for the Trumpet Call

I wrote previously that in a vision I saw myself in my wedding gown. Throughout the Scripture, we see how we obtain that gown by living with the Word and according to the Word, and this brings me to my last point.

This is something very necessary, even essential, to live by. It is found in 2 Timothy 4:8: *"Now there is in store for me the crown of righteousness, which the Lord, the righteous*

Judge will award to me on that day, and not alone to me but also to all who have longed for His appearing."

Hebrews 9:28 also says that Jesus will appear a second time, not to bear sin but to bring full salvation to those who are waiting for Him. The Amplified version of the same verse says: *"To those who are eagerly, constantly and patiently waiting for and expecting Him"* We see here the necessity of always be on our guard and eagerly desire the coming of Jesus in the air. *"For the Lord Himself will come down from heaven, with a loud command and with the voice of the archangel and with the trumpet call of God and be caught up in the clouds to meet the Lord in the air and to be with Him forever" (1 Thess. 4:13–18).*

Word of Wisdom

When I had finished writing the above, the Lord came heavily upon me and gave me a word of wisdom about being a wise virgin and this is what I understood He said:

> *There is a connection between the wise and the foolish virgins and the wise and foolish builders. The wise builders are building their lives with the riches of the Word of God and are standing strong on the eternal Rock.*
>
> *The foolish builders build their lives with the riches of this world, and they will end up in a great crash!*

A Humble, A Longing, And An Expecting Heart

> *The wise virgins filled themselves with the oil of heaven, the Eternal Spirit, and the door was opened to them.*
>
> *The foolish virgins filled themselves with the spirit and pleasures of this world, which are temporal, and the door was shut!*

We, as the bride of Christ, with a longing in our hearts for the coming of our Bridegroom, must continually fill ourselves with the Spirit through our intimacy with Jesus and His Word. Then our lamps will be burning until Jesus comes, as He says, *"Arise, come My darling My beautiful one, and come with Me"* (Song of Songs. 2:10).

Author's Note and Practical Tips

As I said before, this part of being the bride of Christ is most precious to me, and I hope that you can grasp with me, the honor and the glory that is waiting for you in heaven as the bride of Christ. Whether we are going to the Lord before the rapture or in the rapture, the Lord is preparing us throughout our lives to be on His side forever. It is Jesus' deepest desire, yes His intense longing to have His bride on His side. Jesus is also eagerly waiting for that moment. Think about this: He has been waiting already for 2000 years to have all His chosen ones with Him. *In heaven we are His bride and on earth we are His trophy.*

We Are *Trophies* Of *Christ's Victory*

Maybe by reading my stories you will understand why you went through those hardships, pain and difficulties, and see that in those times the Lord in His deep love has never let you go.

Becoming a trophy of Christ's victory will not come by itself, as we also see in the life of Jesus. Through His suffering, Jesus conquered Satan, and because of that victory He has given you also to be victorious over any attack of Satan. Together, with His grace you can stand your battles against all the enemy throws at you. I have seen this over and over in my own life and also in my husband's life. *Remember we are His trophies!!!*

In conclusion, I'd like to give you some practical tips you can remember from my experiences:

- Take time with the Lord and His Word every day, and try to quiet yourself before Him in order to hear His voice.
- Ask the Lord every day for the Spirit of wisdom and revelation, and pray for visions and His divine direction. Visions are very helpful in understanding what the Lord is doing or is going to do in your life. Most of the time He gives it a month or two before it comes to pass, but I have even seen things years before they came to pass. Visions are prophetic. I have seen visions about my husband, which in the natural were scary, but, when I understood that

A Humble, A Longing, And An Expecting Heart

I have to interpret those spiritually, they made much sense, and we have seen them come to fulfilment before our eyes. To interpret visions is also a learning process, but you will also understand and see what those visions mean through knowing the Bible. Everything the Lord gives is spiritual and it will work out in the natural.

- I urge you to create a journal; write down what the Lord is telling you in your heart or revealing to you. Even If you are not sure whether He is speaking to you or you think that you are making it up yourself, write it down anyway. I have thought many times that I was making it up myself but found out later it was the Lord speaking to me. Just write it down, and later you will be surprised to see a pattern in what the Lord is showing you. You will see things fitting together. Other times you will find out the things you thought were right but were not from the Lord, well just dismiss them. It is a learning process, and believe me, you keep on learning through time and experience. And even then, you will find out you will still keep on learning. It never stops until we are with the Lord.

- Be filled with the Spirit, and if you are not baptized in the Holy Spirit, ask the Lord for it and if it doesn't come instantly keep asking! He will fill you to overflowing. Praying, speaking or singing in tongues will open your senses in understanding the realm of the Spirit.

We Are *Trophies* Of *Christ's Victory*

- Eagerly desire to function in the spiritual gifts, especially the gifts that build up the church and God's people. Sometimes I get ideas in my heart and write them down, but at the moment I have no clue what they mean. Then, later on, it becomes clear, and I can see what the Lord was telling me. When we are dedicated to the Lord, He will reveal His will and plan for you.
- God will equip you with everything good for doing His will, and may work in you what is pleasing to Him, through Jesus Christ (see Hebrews 13:21).
- Write down the scriptures that speak to you because God is speaking through His Word. The Word is your life line to heaven. Put those notes on your fridge or mirror where you will be reminded of them all the time. When you get acquainted with those words and get them settled in your heart, they will become alive to you.
- *Hold on to your first love and know the Lord is working out everything for good. You are Christ's trophy, and He is preparing you to be His bride.*

While I was writing the notes above, I experienced in my heart that instead of a prayer I have to do what Paul said to the Ephesian elders. (see Acts 20:32).

> *I am dedicating and committing you to God and to the Word of grace, which can build*

A Humble, A Longing, And An Expecting Heart

you up and give you an inheritance among all those who are sanctified.

Some encouraging short and powerful scriptures I proclaimed in the heavenlies many times for myself and I still do. I am alive because of the Word of God.

John 6:63—The words I have spoken to you are Spirit and they are Life.

Exodus 15:26—For I am the Lord Who heals you.

Psalm 107:20—God sent forth His Word and healed them.

James 5:15—The prayer of Faith shall save the sick, and the Lord shall raise him up.

Mark 11:22—Have faith in God.

Jeremiah 30:17—But I will restore you to health and heal your wounds, declares the Lord.

Psalm 62:1—My soul finds rest in God alone.

Deuteronomy 30:19—Therefore choose life.

Psalm 118:17—I shall not die, but live and declare the works of the Lord.

Isaiah 41:10—Fear not, for I am with you.

Romans 9:33—The one who trust in Him will never be put to shame.

1 Peter 2:24—By His wounds you have been healed.

James 4:7—Submit yourselves to God, resist the devil, and he will flee from you.

1 John 4:4—Greater is He that is in you, than he that is in the world.

Philippians 4:4—Rejoice in the Lord always. I will say again: Rejoice!

Philippians 4:6—Do not be anxious about anything.

Ephesians 6:10—Be strong in the Lord and in His mighty power.

John 14:6—I am the Way and the Truth and the Life.

Isaiah 54:17—No weapon formed against you will prevail.

Psalm 46:10—Be still and know that I am God.

Psalm 63:3—My lips will glorify You.

A Humble, A Longing, And An Expecting Heart

Jeremiah 1:12—I am alert and active watching over My Word to perform it.

Psalm 3:3—But You are a shield around me, O Lord.

Revelation 22:17—The Spirit and the bride say, "Come!

1 Corinthians 15:57—But thanks be to God! He gives us the victory through our Lord Jesus Christ.

2 Corinthians 2:14—But thanks be to God. Who in Christ always leads us in triumph as trophies of Christ's victory.

When you trust and stand on the Word of God, He will never fail you!!!

To contact Ineke Vandewetering: E-mail address:
authorineke@gmail.com